Vietnam's most beloved, aromatic comfort food is now within your reach.

Author Andrea Nguyen first tasted pho in Vietnam as a child, sitting at a Saigon street stall with her parents. That experience sparked a lifelong love of the iconic noodle soup, long before it became a cult food item in the United States. Here Andrea dives deep into pho's lively past, visiting its birthplace and then teaching you how to successfully make it at home.

Options range from quick weeknight cheats to impressive weekend feasts with broth and condiments from scratch, as well as other pho rice noodle favorites. More than fifty versatile recipes, including snacks, salads, companion dishes, and vegetarian and gluten-free options, welcome everyone to the pho table.

With a thoughtful guide on ingredients and techniques, plus evocative location photography and deep historical knowledge, *The Pho Cookbook* enables you to make this comforting classic your own.

ANDREA QUYNHGIAO NGUYEN

STUDIO PHOTOGRAPHY BY JOHN LEE
LOCATION PHOTOGRAPHY BY KAREN SHINTO

THE
PHO
COOKBOOK

EASY TO ADVENTUROUS RECIPES FOR
Vietnam's favorite soup and noodles

TEN SPEED PRESS
BERKELEY

What is Pho?

Pho is so elemental to Vietnamese culture that people talk about it in terms of romantic relationships. Rice is the dutiful wife that you can rely on, we say. Pho is the flirty mistress that you slip away to visit.

I once asked my parents about this comparison. My dad shook his hips to illustrate the mistress. My mom laughed and quipped, "Pho is fun but you can't have it every day. You would get bored. All things in moderation."

The soup first seduced me in 1974, when I perched on a wooden bench at my parents' favorite pho joint and wielded chopsticks and spoon with dexterity and determination. The shop owners marveled; mom and dad beamed with pride. The fragrant broth, savory beef, and springy rice noodles captivated me as I emptied the bowl. I was five years old and suddenly hooked on soup. That experience is among the most vivid from my childhood in Vietnam.

After we immigrated to the States in 1975, there were no neighborhood pho shops to frequent in San Clemente, California, where my family resettled. My pho forays were often homemade, for Sunday brunch.

Like many Vietnamese expatriates, we began savoring pho as a very special food, a gateway to our cultural roots. My mother regularly brewed beef or chicken pho broth on Saturday, then the next morning after eight o'clock mass, we sped home. Everyone had a job on Mom's pho assembly line.

At the table, our bowls of homemade pho were accompanied by fresh chile slices and a few mint sprigs. The simplicity reflected my parents' upbringing in northern Vietnam, where purity prevailed. They'd lived in liberal Saigon (now Ho Chi Minh City) for decades, but they didn't allow embellishments like bean sprouts, Thai basil, or lime wedges. And definitely no sriracha, which Mom deemed un-Vietnamese.

As a college student in Los Angeles, I went to pho restaurants that served up giant bowls with plates piled high with produce for personalizing flavors. Flummoxed at first, I learned to loosen up, even at the sight of someone squirting hoisin and sriracha into a bowl. Over the years, I practiced making my own pho, developed recipes for my first cookbook, *Into the Vietnamese Kitchen* (2006), researched pho in Vietnam and wrote articles on it, answered reporter and blogger queries, and taught pho classes to countless cooks.

Interest in pho has risen exponentially as it has moved from the margins to the mainstream. It's a favorite food for many but it's also been the focus of novels, art exhibits, rap songs, and Kickstarter campaigns. People are smitten by Vietnam's signature dish for many reasons: Pho is comforting (noodles in clear broth satisfy), healthy (there's little fat and gluten), restorative (try it for colds and hangovers), and friendly (you can have it your way). It's also delicious.

I figured that I knew what pho was all about until friends, Facebook fans, and then my publisher suggested that I write a pho cookbook. Seriously? What was there to present beyond the familiar brothy bowl? As it turned out, a lot. It didn't take me long to realize that the world of pho was unusually rich with culinary and cultural gems.

ORIGINAL PHO

Vietnam is a country with a history spanning over thirty-five hundred years, but pho is a relatively new food. It's unclear how and when it was birthed, though most people agree that the magical moment happened at the beginning of the twentieth century in and near Hanoi, the capital located in the northern part of the country.

Prior to 1910, images of pho street food vendors appeared in *Technique du Peuple Annamite (Mechanics and Crafts of the People of Annam*, 1908–1910), a multivolume effort by Henri J. Oger. He was a colonial administrator who commissioned artisans and wood carvers to document life in Hanoi and the surrounding countryside.

But what was the source of the original pho? Some say that long before pho got popularized, it was being prepared in Van Cu, an impoverished village in Nam Dinh Province located about sixty miles (one hundred kilometers) southeast of Hanoi. The village and province produced generations of pho masters, many of whom relocated to the capital to open well-regarded pho shops.

In October 2015, I ventured to look for myself; details of the mini pho expedition are on page 14.

We'll likely never know for certain how pho first came about, but it's in great company: almost all beloved foods have origin controversies that fuel conversations and imaginations. What's clear is that pho was created from cultures rubbing shoulders.

There are many theories, but a reasonable explanation for pho was presented in "100 Năm Phở Việt" ("100 Years of Vietnamese Pho," 2010), an oft-cited historical essay by Dung Quang Trinh. In the Hanoi area during the early 1900s, there was a lot of interaction between the Vietnamese, French, and Chinese (China and Vietnam are next-door neighbors). The French, who officially occupied Vietnam from the 1880s to 1954, satiated their desires for tender steaks by slaughtering cows, which the Vietnamese traditionally used as draft animals. The leftover bones and scraps were salvaged and sold by a handful of Hanoi butchers.

Locals hadn't yet developed a taste for beef, and the butchers had to promote it via special deals and sales. Street vendors who were already selling noodle soup recognized an opportunity to offer something new. It was just a matter of switching the menu of their portable kitchens.

At that time, a noodle soup called *xáo trâu* was very popular. It was simply made, with slices of water buffalo served in broth with rice vermicelli. The vendors swapped beef for water buffalo. Somewhere in the process, they also traded flat rice noodles for the round rice vermicelli.

The result was a noodle soup that some people called *xáo bò*, but since many of the vendors were Chinese, the Vietnamese-Cantonese name prevailed: *ngưu nhục phấn* (beef with rice noodles). Viet culture and language were in flux when pho emerged on the scene.

The new noodle soup was often prepared and sold by food hawkers who roamed the streets looking for customers. Many of the initial pho customers were Chinese coolies and other workers whose livelihoods were tied to the French and Chinese merchant ships that sailed up and down the Red River; the river flowed from Yunnan Province, past the edge of Hanoi, then into the Gulf of Tonkin, connecting a diverse group of people.

French and Chinese merchant ships employed many Yunnanese, who likely identified *ngưu nhục phấn* as being akin to Yunnan's *guò qiáo mǐ xiàn* (crossing the bridge noodles), composed of rice noodles, superhot broth, meat, and vegetables. The beef noodle soup caught on with the Chinese workers and, soon thereafter, with the many ethnic Vietnamese who began working on the river, too.

The popularity of the dish spread as the number of street food vendors rose in response to Hanoi's colonial urbanization, according to historian Erica Peters. The initial pho shops opened in the bustling Old Quarter (the main commercial hub) and more followed. Nam Dinh–style pho shops seeded their reputation around 1925, when a skilled cook from Van Cu opened a storefront in Hanoi. By 1930, pho could be found in many parts of the city.

How did *ngưu nhục phấn* become *phở*? It is likely that as the dish caught on, street hawkers became more competitive and abbreviated their distinctive calls. For example, "Ngưu nhục phấn đây" (Beef and rice noodles here) was shortened to "Ngưu phấn a," then "Phấn a" or "Phốn ơ," and finally settled into one word, *phở*. It's been suggested that *phở* won because if *phấn* is mispronounced or misheard as *phân*, it would mean "excrement."

In a Vietnamese language dictionary published around 1930, an entry for *phở* defined it as a dish of narrowly sliced noodles and beef, its name having been derived from *phấn*, the Viet pronunciation of *fẽn*, the Chinese term for flat rice noodle. Despite the Viet-Chinese definition, some people have conjectured that the term is French in origin because its pronunciation bears a resemblance to *feu* ("fire" in French), as in *pot-au-feu*, the boiled beef dinner. The terms indeed sound similar, and pho came about during the French colonial period, but it's difficult to accept that the soup directly descended from French cuisine. Pho doesn't involve lots of vegetables like *pot-au-feu* does, for example. A plausible Franco-Viet connection is the technique of charring ginger and onion or shallot for pho broth (see page 30).

No one may claim pho but the Vietnamese because it happened on Vietnamese soil under a unique set of circumstances. It was genius make-do cooking. While

HOW TO SAY PHO LIKE A NATIVE

Since *phở* officially entered the Oxford and Merriam-Webster dictionaries in 2006 and 2014, respectively, it is no longer a foreign term requiring accent marks or italics. Hooray! However, the simplified spelling of pho may mislead people about how to pronounce it. A little background on Vietnamese language will help you figure out how to say the word and impress a native speaker.

Word	Accent Mark	Pronunciation
Pho	None	"faww"
Phơ	Side hook on the last letter	"fuh"
Phở	Side hook plus question mark	"fuhh?"

Remember the little question mark above the letter *o* and say pho with confidence.

original pho was a simple bowl of broth, noodles, and boiled beef, as time went on, cooks began experimenting with different techniques and ingredients, some of which were influenced by other cultures and others that were spurred on by necessity. In the late 1920s, people debated the merits of pho featuring spices similar to those in Chinese five-spice powder, peanut oil, tofu, and *cà cuống* (a pear-scented water beetle pheromone). Vendors were serving up pho with rare beef slices by 1930. Around that time, *phở xào dòn*, panfried pho rice noodles topped with a saucy beef and vegetable stir-fry, was introduced and well received; see recipes in the chapter on stir-fried, panfried, and deep-fried pho dishes starting on page 113.

Things got heated in 1939 when pho restaurants began selling chicken pho (*phở gà*). It usually happened on Mondays and Fridays and was likely due to the government forbidding the sale of beef on those days in order to control the slaughtering of draft animals for food. Purists initially decried chicken pho as being un-pho-like, but in the end, it prevailed as a worthy and tasty preparation in its own right. In fact, some pho shops decided to specialize in *phở gà*.

One last note about terminology: *phở* not only refers to the noodle soup but is also shorthand for the dish's flat rice noodles, *bánh phở*. The word's dual culinary meanings are telling. Pho is not only about the soup but also about the rice noodle and its many glorious manifestations.

PROTEST AND POLITICAL PHO

Foreign occupation, civil war, the Vietnam War, reunification, and rebuilding—the twentieth century was tumultuous for Vietnam. Pho got swept up in the events that unfolded.

During the 1930s, many authors and poets in Hanoi resisted the French occupation with their pens. In 1934, one of the country's distinguished poets, Tu Mo, published *Phở Đức Tụng* (*An Ode to Pho*). A nationalistic satirist, Tu Mo wanted to convey Viet pride and people's desire for justice and self-determination. After espousing the unique deliciousness of pho, how it arouses the senses, and how its bone broth nourishes rich and poor as well as artists, singers, and prostitutes, he concluded with these lines, which I have loosely translated:

> **Don't downgrade pho by labeling it a humble food,**
> **Even the city of Paris has to welcome pho.**
> **Compared to other international foods of note,**
> **It is delicious yet inexpensive and is often crowned the best.**
> **Living in this world without eating pho is foolish,**
> **Upon death, the altar offerings should include it.**
> **Now go savor pho, or you shall crave it.**

When the French colonial period ended in 1954 and the Geneva Accords split the country into North and South Vietnam, about one million northerners migrated southward, heralding the arrival of Hanoi-style pho to

Saigon. Saigonese were familiar with pho by 1950, but proud northerners like my mother say that pho wasn't popularized there until they showed up. (Restaurants abroad named "Pho 1954" often give a nod to that important marker in Vietnamese history and cuisine.)

In the agriculturally rich and freewheeling south, pho broth eventually developed a sweet edge, as cooks added a touch of Chinese rock sugar. Southerners also liked a lot of accessories: bean sprouts, Thai basil, chile sauce, and a hoisin-like fermented bean sauce. Northerners were aghast. The new additions desecrated their well-balanced, delicate soup. To this day, the regional pho fight between Hanoi and Saigon—north versus south, salty versus sweet, simple versus eclectic—rages on.

The late 1950s were cruel to pho in Hanoi. The Communist Party nationalized many businesses for the sake of social reform. The Soviet Union sent economic aid, including a lot of potato starch and wheat flour. Xuan Phuong, a former party loyalist, recounted that era's pho experience in her compelling 2004 memoir, *Ao Dai: My War, My Country, My Vietnam*.

The government restricted "real" pho because it wasted precious rice, she explained, and the resulting state-run pho shops produced bowls of "rotten rice noodles, a little bit of tough meat, and a tasteless broth." People who could afford pho lined up for it nevertheless, only to face unhygienic conditions (chopsticks were seldom washed) and suffer humiliation (holes were pierced in spoons to prevent people from stealing them). Pho street vendors were limited to selling soup with potato starch noodles. Hanoians determined to get good pho found a work-around, as she described:

Little by little, the rules were overlooked. To deceive controllers, the street merchants placed a small basket of those shriveled up noodles on display. But the pho, the real stuff, was underneath. It was almost as good as it had used to be and hardly more expensive than the substitute. We all passed on our list of secret addresses. "I would like a bowl of soup with potato flour noodles," we would say out loud, just in case any State officials were hanging around. The merchant would understand immediately. But then the pho had to be downed very quickly to keep the unfortunate man or woman from having his or her equipment seized, as well as a fine to pay.

During the Vietnam War, a different kind of pho underground operated in Saigon. Starting around 1965, a Viet Cong spy cell operated out of Pho Binh (literally "Peace Noodles"). The seven-table joint was a communist nerve center for carrying out the city's part in the 1968 Tet Offensive. According to a 2010 *Los Angeles Times* article, Pho Binh was a hub for organizing and transporting weapons from northern strongholds to secret hiding places in Saigon.

Elsewhere in the city, people tried to maintain calm and normal lives. Many headed to "pho streets" such as Ly Thai To and Pasteur for satisfying bowls at popular restaurants like Pho Hoa and Pho Tau Bay.

In Hanoi, wartime scarcity forced state-run pho shops to make the soup without meat. In 1964, after the United States began sending unmanned reconnaissance planes to photograph North Vietnam, locals mockingly called their meager soup *phở không người lái*, literally "pho without a pilot." A bowl of pho noodle soup is defined by its protein (you order pho by the cuts of beef or chicken), and meatless pho seemed as surreal, if not as absurd, as a drone aircraft.

Wartime pho in Hanoi was often served inappropriately, namely with leftover cold rice and baguette. Fried breadsticks called *bánh quẩy* were the saving grace; they were procured from Chinese vendors who spotted an opportunity to inject richness into an otherwise sad pho experience. The breadsticks (page 109) became a local pho accompaniment that endures today in the capital.

My cousin Huy Do Le, a Hanoi native in his late fifties, recalled the state-run pho shops producing deplorable soup, whereas street pho operators were much better. He and a friend, poet Giang Van, lived through those hard times, as well as the lean years after the Vietnam War ended in 1975. The nation was reunified as one, but its economy was in shambles. Food was rationed and people stood in line for nearly everything, including pho. One midmorning over tea, they wistfully discussed their longing for the elegant simplicity of Hanoi foodways: smallish portions of flat rice noodles, savory yet slightly sweet broth, and sliced cooked beef. "No fried breadsticks, condiments, or other extra things. Traditional Hanoi style is pure and delicate," Giang Van said.

Saigonese continue to celebrate pho with all of the embellishments because that's how they like it. For people who experienced extra hardship, there's a smidgen of defiance, too. During a pho breakfast in Saigon, I asked my cousin Phu Si Nguyen, an energetic retired teacher in his seventies, about pho after the Communist takeover in April 1975. "My brother and I were jailed, sent to reeducation camps," he said with a wry smile. "Times were difficult, but now, there is plenty of good pho in Saigon." We all nodded, added bean sprouts and herbs to our bowls, and dug in.

CULINARY AND CULTURAL PHO

Pho is about tradition as much as it is about change. It comforts as well as stokes the imagination.

While beef pho remains the favorite and chicken pho ranks second in terms of popularity, Vietnamese cooks are always coming up with something new. Some dishes, like pho with beef stewed in white wine (*phở sốt vang*) and sour pho (*phở chua*), never totally caught on, whereas Fresh Pho Noodle Rolls (page 133) were a hit.

WHAT IS VIET?

For Vietnamese people, the term *Việt* signals nationalism and resistance to foreign domination. Used by Vietnamese speakers to describe anything Vietnamese (like Thai for Thailand), Viet was originally the Chinese term for the various peoples living on the southern fringes of the Han empire. The maverick kingdom of Nam Viet fought Chinese rule in the second century BC. Under Chinese and French control, Viet was absent from names applied to Vietnamese territory. The term reemerged during periods of independence to express Vietnamese self-determination. Given the term's significance, Viet and Vietnamese are used interchangeably in this book.

As interest in Vietnamese food and travel rises, there's incredible excitement about pho. In Hanoi, family-owned, multigenerational pho shops do a brisk business with traditionalists, while young people are keen on nontraditional preparations such as Chicken Pho Noodle Salad (page 75) and Deep-Fried Pho Noodles (page 120). Souvenir vendors in the historic Old Quarter sell pho T-shirts and postcards. Tourists and street food tours include pho on their bucket lists. The esteemed Hotel Sofitel Legend Metropole has a pho cocktail on its menu (see page 150).

In Saigon, where there are pho concerns large and small, happy customers slurp away morning, noon, and night. Tourists flock to Pho 2000, where former president Bill Clinton ate, while locals patronize favorites such as Pho Le and Pho Hoa. Arty and modern Ru Pho Bar presents pho made with brown rice noodles. Customers at Pho Hai Thien may order pho with a rainbow of noodles tinted by vegetable juices. Pho tchotchkes are sold on the streets as well as at the airport.

Outside of the motherland, pho has taken root wherever there are Vietnamese people. Its strongholds include North America, France, and Australia, where many immigrants have settled and built thriving Little Saigon enclaves. Whether they were born in Vietnam or abroad, people of Viet ancestry are reinforcing their cultural roots through pho, opening and patronizing small joints in their communities, cooking up their own at home, and introducing the noodle soup to friends. Nowadays, Viet-owned restaurants present traditional broths and freshly made *bánh phở* noodles, but also try out new ideas, such as crawfish pho, sous vide–beef pho, and pho fried rice.

Mainstream supermarkets in the United States carry pho kits and instant pho bowls. Non-Vietnamese chefs are serving pho in restaurants while home cooks try their hands at making it themselves. The widespread availability of fish sauce and rice noodles at supermarkets, ethnic grocers, and online makes DIY pho doable.

The future of pho shines very bright. Let's get started with making some.

IS PHO ONLY FOR BREAKFAST?

The Viet breakfast of champions is a bowl of pho paired with coffee mixed with condensed milk. It's a fabulous wake-up call that energizes and satisfies. Many traditional pho shops in Vietnam open in the morning, serve their daily batch, and close around midmorning. Some reopen at night and others are open all day long. Lunchtime pho breaks up the day nicely. Late-night pho is a fun chaser after a light supper. Go ahead and eat pho when the mood strikes you.

VISITING THE "BIRTHPLACE" OF PHO

Getting good pho in Vietnam sometimes requires a very early start. On a 2015 trip to Hanoi, I woke up around 5:30 a.m. to journey to the purported birthplace of pho. Local food experts Tracey Lister, Duyen Thi Phan, and Mark Lowerson joined me and my colleague, Karen Shinto. Mark arranged for Dan Tran, a plucky local guide, to drive and be our fixer.

"Why are we going to Nam Dinh and Van Cu?" Dan asked, somewhat bewildered.

"Because Wikipedia says that that's where pho may have originated," I responded.

We all chuckled, but actually, among diehard pho lovers, Nam Dinh and Van Cu signal a well-crafted, northern-style pho. People from the province, which includes its namesake capital city and Van Cu village, are responsible for many good pho shops. In fact, in *Pho: A Specialty of Ha Noi* (2006), editors Huu Ngoc and Lady Borton wrote that the Association of Van Cu Residents in Hanoi claimed that about 80 percent of the city's pho shops had roots in the village.

Fueled by coffee and excitement, we chatted practically nonstop during the 1½-hour drive, but upon entering the city proper, we fell silent. Nam Dinh had graceful, wide avenues. Things were calm, traffic moved in an orderly fashion, pedestrians crossed the streets with ease. It was refreshing compared to bustling Hanoi.

Dan cruised to find pho shops on our hit list. Not one was open. It was close to nine o'clock when he parked near a cluster of businesses, and we fanned out to query locals. One renowned spot had permanently shuttered, a woman told Duyen and Tracey; the owners had moved their operations to Hanoi. Another person offered the new address of a good pho shop, but when we arrived, it was closing.

"We are done for the day," the owner said. "Come back tomorrow around seven o'clock."

We traveled from Hanoi, I pleaded. Dan explained our pho expedition and asked if there was anything to sample. The owner shook his head. Maybe we could call ahead next time, Dan suggested.

The owner gruffly said, "When we are in service, we are busy. No one has time to pick up the phone! You have to come back."

His resolute attitude echoed the old-timey quality of the shop. He'd sold out of everything produced from his coal-fired stove. Orderly stacks of cleaned bowls and condiment setups had been readied for the next day.

We headed to Van Cu village, past rice paddies, roadside pho shops, and villages marked by ornate church spires. A rustic building with "Pho" painted in large, red letters announced that we were near our destination. At the turnoff to the village, Mark spotted a closed pho shop that claimed relation to a pho shop in Hanoi. The birthplace of pho was incredibly low key.

Through a villager, Dan confirmed the location of a pho noodle maker, and we snaked our way through the narrow passageways. The noodle maker's home was the biggest and best appointed. The family welcomed us once they understood our unusual purpose.

I fantasized that the noodles would be made by hand but that was ridiculous. The family-owned factory made noodles by machine, with a conveyor belt that steamed the batter into thin sheets, which were then machine cut, gathered by hand, and hung to cool. They used to grind the soaked rice by hand, one young man explained. When an electric stone grinder became available, they gladly switched.

To underscore the family's wealth and success, the matriarch invited me to visit with her happy, healthy pigs. "They are fed leftover rice noodles," she proudly shared.

We had set out that morning expecting to experience pho in its full brothy glory. Not tasting it was a letdown but also a valuable lesson on how it endures as a favorite Vietnamese breakfast food. The triumph of the day was meeting the people of Nam Dinh and Van Cu. Their humble hospitality and craftsmanship has fed the global pho phenomenon so incredibly well.

1

PHO MANUAL

In the Viet food world, pho carries two meanings: a bowl of noodle soup and flat rice noodles. This book explores that broad understanding, and to work smoothly through the recipes, you must first peruse this chapter.

Much of the information is geared toward pho noodle soup because that's the ballast for your food adventure to come. The ingredient guide explains what you need and why you need it, as well as how to source it. There's information on equipment and dishware, too. Glean the pho soup tips to develop and perfect your skills. The manual supports the five recipe chapters.

Master Pho contains foundational recipes for preparing pho at your own pace and schedule. **Adventurous Pho** pushes the limits a bit to inspire your pho creativity. **Pho Add-Ons** offers guidance on extra toppings, garnishes, and sauces so that you may personalize your pho. **Stir-Fried, Panfried, and Deep-Fried Pho** makes the most of wide pho noodles. **Pho Sidekicks** includes rolls, dumplings, salads, and drinks to help you plan a special pho meal.

Timing and advanced prep tips are tucked into the recipes throughout. Be sure to read the recipe introductions and Notes sections for extra details. If you make an adjustment, write it down for future batches.

Alongside the standard American measuring system are metric equivalents. With the exception of the Fried Breadsticks dough (page 109), and Fresh Pho Noodle Rolls batter (page 133), the metric equivalents are stated as practical figures, that is, rounded off so that 16 ounces is 450 grams instead of 454 grams, and 1 ounce is 30 grams instead of 28.35 grams.

These recipes will not be ruined if you're not 100 percent on the mark. Have a sense of your goal and get into the pho spirit.

Dried Rice Noodles

WIDE

NARROW

PAD THAI OR BÁNH PHỞ

CHOW FUN

Fresh Rice Noodles

VACUUM PACKED

INGREDIENTS

Making pho is not challenging. What's needed is likely at your fingertips. Mine the Asian, ethnic food, and bulk spice sections at supermarkets, natural foods markets, and retailers like Cost Plus World Market. However, for great deals on noodles and fish sauce or unusual ingredients such as rock sugar, shop at a Chinese or Vietnamese market. Depending on the recipe, purchase the best chicken, beef, seafood, and vegetables that you can afford. They give their all to define the pho. Your investment will yield stunning dividends. Look to recipe introductions and notes for specific tips.

Below are the most-often-used ingredients in this book. They're presented in order of importance and sometimes grouped in a category (for example, spices) to help you prioritize and understand their functions.

Water

Don't neglect the water, a major broth ingredient that matters. Brew the broth with water that you enjoy drinking. Soaking noodles and other prep tasks can be done with regular tap water.

Noodles

Rice noodles carry and convey pho flavor. Made by steaming rice batter into thin sheets and then cutting them into strands, *bánh phở* rice noodles define pho soup. Note that *bánh phở* are flat rice noodles, whereas round *bún* rice vermicelli noodles are used for other dishes, including Rice Paper Salad Rolls (page 135).

Flat rice noodles are sold in different widths to match cooking applications; they are used in Vietnamese, Thai, and Chinese cuisines and thus marketed for popular dishes like pho, pad Thai, and *chow fun*. There is no standard for the sizing, but for the purposes of this book, I've split them into two categories: **Narrow rice noodles** (linguine or fettuccine size) are perfect for pho noodle soup. **Wide rice noodles** (think pappardelle) work best for the stir-fried, panfried, and deep-fried noodles.

Pho noodles are available fresh and dried. In Vietnam, fresh noodles are relatively easy to obtain, but people use dried ones, too. Abroad, the situation is reversed: most cooks prepare dried noodles and occasionally get fresh ones. Don't worry, because the dried ones have a terrific chewiness that's practically as good as fresh. There is a difference in how dried and fresh noodles are used in the recipes. For pho noodle soup, see page 32. For stir-fried, panfried, and deep-fried dishes, see the recipes starting on page 113. Following is a summary of your noodle options.

Dried rice noodles are easy to find and to store for later use.

Availability: Find these noodles at supermarkets and natural foods markets in the Asian or international food section, Chinese and Vietnamese markets in the dried noodle aisle, and Cost Plus World Market in the Asian food section.

Packaging: Look for boxes or plastic packages of rice sticks, pad Thai noodles, *bánh phở*, or Chantaboon (a Thai city renowned for rice noodles).

Sizes: Narrow noodles are labeled "S" (linguine) and "M" (fettuccine). Wide noodles are marked "L" or "XL" (pappardelle).

Reliable brands: Seek out Annie Chun's, Three Ladies, Caravelle, and Bangkok Elephant. If possible, try different brands and pick a favorite. Some are thin and delicate, while others are thick and chewy.

Selection tips: Choose packages with the least number of broken noodles. Most rice noodles are made from white rice. Brown rice noodles are good; purple and red rice noodles are striking but cook up soft.

Storage: Store in the cupboard and use them within a year of purchase. As with dried pasta, keep partially opened packages in a zipper plastic bag (so they remain neat) or transfer to a tall storage container.

Fresh rice noodles offer an extra-authentic, tender-chewy treat, but they are more difficult to source and don't last long.

Availability: Locate these noodles at Chinese and Vietnamese markets in the refrigerated sections, near egg noodles and dumpling wrappers.

Packaging: Vacuum-packed *bánh phở tươi* (fresh pho noodles, fresh rice stick noodles) are located in the chiller case. Nearby and unrefrigerated may be a display of superfresh, soft rice noodles; they're unchilled to preserve their just-made texture. They may be labeled *bánh phở*, pad Thai noodles, or *chow fun*.

Sizes: Chilled vacuum-packed rice noodles are usually small (linguine). Unchilled *bánh phở* or pad Thai noodles are usually medium (fettuccine). And *chow fun* are large (pappardelle).

Reliable brands: Pick a market that you trust. It should sell the best brand(s) to its customers.

Selection tips: Vacuum-packed noodles should have a sealed, tight appearance. Superfresh noodles should be soft (poke to test).

Storage: Vacuum-packed noodles keep well in the fridge for about 10 days; once opened, use within 3 days. Superfresh noodles are best used the day of purchase but will keep refrigerated for 5 days.

Spices

A blend of spices contributes aroma and flavor to create a multidimensional pho broth. Typical spices are warm and sweet, but each has its individual personality. In a respectable pho broth, no one spice hits you over the head. The blend varies from cook to cook, so experiment.

Pho spice notes are strongest in the first seventy-two hours after cooking. If they seem weak or you want to adjust the flavor, bring the strained broth to a boil and add more spices (pick one or two and use about 25 percent of the original amount), turn off the heat, cover, and let steep for 1 hour before removing the spices and finishing the seasoning.

Buy whole spices and keep frozen if your stash is large. Purchase them where there is a quick turnover, such as an Asian market or a natural foods store's bulk spice section. Most pho spices are widely available. Below are spices I use and why.

Star anise (*đại hồi*) defines the broth aroma and flavor with its sweet licorice, slightly bitter notes. Much of the flavor is in the petal-shaped carpels. A whole star anise has about eight of those seed pods (referred to as "points" in recipes). Choose robust points for maximum flavor. Broken star anise is fine.

Chinese black cardamom (*thảo quả*) can challenge with its smoky, woodsy, menthol-like qualities, but some say it's the signature pho flavor. Looking like deeply ridged whole nutmeg, it is sold at Chinese and Viet markets in small plastic packages in the spice section, as well as online. When shopping, look for the Viet spelling (*thảo quả*), the botanical name (*Amomum tsao-ko*), and the Chinese name (*cao guo*). In a pinch, use the weight equivalent in smaller Indian black cardamom. A medium Chinese black cardamom weighs .07 ounce (2 grams) and a very large one weighs .25 ounce (6 grams). Green cardamom is not the same as Chinese black cardamom.

CINNAMON
STICKS

CASSIA BARK

BLACK CARDAMOM

CORIANDER
SEED

FENNEL
SEED

STAR
ANISE

CLOVE

CHINESE YELLOW
ROCK SUGAR

Cinnamon (*quế*) complements star anise and black cardamom via its warm, earthy, zingy traits. Cassia cinnamon, such as Vietnamese "Saigon" cinnamon, is best for building pho flavor; thank goodness it's the variety commonly sold in America. Cinnamon sticks are used in these recipes. When substituting irregular pieces of cassia bark from Asian grocery stores (for comparison, see page 21), weigh it to ensure the quantity used: A slender, medium, and husky cinnamon stick respectively weighs .07 ounce (2 g), .1 ounce (3 g), and .2 ounce (5 g).

Clove (*đinh hương*) plays off star anise and black cardamom, just like cinnamon. The recipes in this book use whole cloves. Select plump ones.

Coriander seeds (*hột ngò*) round things out with their delicate, citrusy personalities. Spherical coriander seeds work well for pho; football-shaped ones are too sweet.

Fennel seeds (*tiểu hồi*) serve a similar purpose to coriander seeds by adding a refreshing sweet lilt.

Pepper (*tiêu*) is often sprinkled onto pho bowls during assembly to add zingy heat. If possible, keep a small jar of freshly ground black pepper in the kitchen. Buy whole peppercorns and use a coffee grinder dedicated to grinding spices. After each use, grind 2 teaspoons raw rice to clean the grinder. White pepper is not used often in this book.

Aromatics

Aromatics, mainly ginger and onion or shallot, lend mellow, sweet heat and pungency to pho broth. Here are general guidelines for selecting and using these important pho ingredients.

Ginger is used heavily in pho. Buy punchy ginger that feels dense for its size. When in doubt, break off a knob: stringy bits usually signal good sweet heat and fragrance. Ginger varies in size and weight; a "chubby" section is as wide as a big toe, and 1 inch (2.5 cm) weighs about 1 ounce (30 g). Use a scale to make sure there is enough. Store ginger unpeeled for weeks in a plastic bag in the refrigerator produce bin.

Shallot and onion are both used for making pho broth. What you choose depends on your circumstance and taste preference. In Vietnam, cooks traditionally favor shallot because it is affordable and lends a certain pungent-sweet edge. Many pho cooks abroad, however, select yellow onion over shallot because the former is less expensive, more accessible, and offers a sweet-pungent note to the broth. Most pho broths in this book employ yellow onion, but you can opt for shallot (see the Hanoi-Style Beef Pho on page 65). Or, try combining shallot and onion in a 1:1 ratio.

For garnishing the soup bowls, choose yellow or red onion; the superhot broth cooks the thin onion slices, releasing last-minute flavor and aroma. (Note that some cooks opt to garnish pho with fried shallots, which skews pho toward southern Vietnamese *hủ tiếu* noodle soup. That practice unnecessarily fusses up the bowl.) Regardless of the application and your decision, select firm, solid-feeling bulbs and keep in a dry spot.

Green onion serves as a last-minute pho soup garnish. In Vietnam, skinny, mild-tasting green onions are cut into long pieces for pho soup. American green onions have more bite, so I only cut the milder green portions when yellow or red onion is also used for garnishing the bowl. For the Hanoi-style pho on page 65, only green onions are used for garnish; all the white and green parts are thinly cut on a very sharp diagonal so they'll be quickly mellowed by the hot broth ladled into the bowl.

Salt

One of the major ingredients for establishing the savory foundation of a pho broth is salt. Fine sea salt yields great broth, is easy to find, and has a consistent weight across brands. The flavor and saltiness varies, so always salt to taste. My go-to sea salt is made by La Baleine. If you prefer table salt, add a lesser amount than what the recipe suggests. Morton's kosher salt users ought to measure about 20 percent *more* in volume than what is called for in the recipes. Diamond Crystal kosher salt fans should double the quantity of salt called for in a recipe in this cookbook. When in doubt, use a little less salt, as you can add more later.

Some cooks like to add an extra savory undercurrent by making broth with dried seafood. See the Hanoi-Style Beef Pho (page 65) for details.

Sweeteners

Several sweetening agents may be used to unite flavors and create a savory-sweet finish in pho broth.

Chinese yellow rock sugar is the go-to sweetener for many pho cooks. It magically helps to round out the jagged edges of the other elements (imagine using sandpaper on a rough surface). Southern-style pho broth often includes rock sugar (*đường phèn*) to make it complete. The mildly sweet nuggets are sold at Asian markets in plastic packages or paper boxes labeled as "yellow rock sugar" or "yellow lump sugar." *Do not* buy flat-tasting white rock sugar. If you find large, Kryptonite-like chunks in your package, wrap them in a lint-free cloth, place on a hard surface (I favor my cement patio), and bang away with a hammer or meat mallet. Store rock sugar in an airtight container at room temperature; it lasts indefinitely. Look for yellow rock

MSG AND OTHER FLAVOR ENHANCERS

The recipes in this book have plenty of salty-savory goodness. If you're curious or feel the need for extra umami bursts, include a flavor enhancer when finishing the broth or add some to each bowl during assembly; the hot broth will distribute the magic.

Monosodium glutamate (MSG) has been consumed by people for more than a hundred years to add oomph and finesse to dishes. In fact, many people consider MSG and other flavor enhancers to be indispensable for perfect pho. They'll employ the fine white crystals or mushroom seasoning granules, an MSG substitute (Po Lo Ku, Imperial Taste, and Takii are reliable brands).

Note that mushroom seasoning is akin to nutritional yeast in that it turns broth cloudy. As a work-around, dissolve 1 tablespoon of the granules in ⅓ cup (90 ml) of hot broth or water. Let sit for about 10 minutes, until separated. Season the broth with the salty, clearer liquid at the top.

Despite what manufacturers say, MSG and mushroom seasoning enhance flavors in distinctive ways. Use them judiciously, as too much will make a dish monochromatic. And avoid MSG if you are prone to reacting to it.

sugar in the flour, sugar, and spice section of a Chinese or Vietnamese market. It's sold online too.

Other sweeteners for pho may be at your fingertips. When a trip to an Asian market isn't possible, use **maple syrup** or **organic cane sugar** and maybe some **Fuji apple**. The maple syrup and organic sugar have character and depth. The apple is a terrific natural source for sweetness. Some cooks add daikon to pho broth, but its flavor varies from mild to bitter-spicy. Fuji apple is more reliable and widely available; to remain in the vegetable realm, try mildly sweet Tokyo turnip in an equal weight.

Seasonings

A savory liquid seasoning typically completes the broth flavor close to when pho is served. You'll come across these seasonings in the soup recipes and elsewhere.

Fish sauce is the default liquid seasoning for most savory Viet dishes, including pho. Use a premium brand of fish sauce (*nước mắm*), such as MegaChef, Red Boat, and Viet Huong/Three Crabs—sold at supermarkets, specialty grocers, and Asian markets. Check ingredient listings if you're gluten sensitive. A touch of sugar in the bottle actually helps to easily dial in the right pho umami note; if the fish sauce lacks sugar, you likely need extra sweetness when seasoning the broth. Refrigerate fish sauce if you don't use it often; should it darken and intensify in flavor, use a little less than usual. Replace the bottle if crystals form.

Soy sauce lends umami to many Viet dishes, including pho broth. For **regular soy sauce**, use Kikkoman or Pearl River Bridge brand. Or, substitute a wheat-free one, such as Kikkoman or Lee Kum Kee brand, which has good flavor partly due to a touch of sugar. Some recipes in this book call for **dark soy sauce** to deepen flavor and color; it's mostly available at Asian markets, but you may use the work-around suggested in the instructions. Store soy sauce in a cool, dry cupboard.

Maggi Seasoning sauce injects a unique meaty flavor to meatless pho broth. At supermarkets, look for Maggi near browning sauces and gravy enhancers or with Latin and Asian foods. Chinese and Viet grocers shelve it with the soy sauces; Viet delis and bakeries usually carry it, too. The standard Chinese version is robust and good for cooking. Bragg Liquid Aminos is a less salty substitute, so use a bit extra.

Nutritional yeast is used to create the savory, chicken-like vegetarian broth on page 53. Purchase the yellow powder or flakes at natural foods markets (check bulk bins and the spice aisle). Store it in the cupboard.

Herbs

Fresh herbs perfume and flavor pho just before it touches your lips. The three most-often-used ones follow. See the Garnish Plate recipe (page 100) for other herb options. In this book, pho herbs are used not only for pho soup but also in fried rice, salads, and other recipes.

Cilantro is a classic herb for garnishing pho bowls. Trim about ½ inch (1.25 cm) from the ends of a bunch, then put the bunch in a container partially filled with water. Loosely cover with a plastic produce bag and refrigerate. Change the water every 2 or 3 days and the cilantro will remain perky for about 7 days. Once washed and spun dry in a salad spinner, cilantro can be stored in a zipper plastic bag for several days. If you omit cilantro, add mint or Thai basil at the table.

Mint is a pho herb that's overlooked in the West. Offered at the table, it lends a bright note to pho. Spearmint (what is commonly sold) is great for pho. Store it just like cilantro, or grow it!

Thai basil thrives in hot weather and may be purchased at Southeast Asian and Chinese markets. Refrigerate it as is on the Styrofoam tray from the market or slide into a thin plastic produce bag; excess moisture ruins the leaves.

Other Garnishes

There are a number of toppings and garnishes used to crown pho, from vegetables and herbs to meats and sauces. Some have already been covered above, and others appear in the recipes. Below are the most common.

Chiles add heat and perfume to spark up a bowl of pho. Maintain a small supply of Thai, jalapeño, Fresno, or serrano in the fridge, where they'll stay fresh for a good week. Thai chiles may be kept frozen for up to a year. See page 100 for details on chile heat vagaries. Unless specified in a recipe, chiles are used with the seeds intact.

Bean sprouts offer textural contrast at the table. When buying bean sprouts in bags, select mung bean sprouts (what's typically sold), not soybean sprouts (which have large yellow beans attached and are hard to digest when raw). The sprouts should look dry and perky, not wet and limp; check the "best by" date for freshness. Wash well in a bowl of water, removing any unsightly dark-colored parts; there's no need to snap off the tips or tails.

Hoisin sauce is incredibly easy to make with the recipe on page 102. If you prefer to buy it, delicate-tasting Lee Kum Kee hoisin is sold at many supermarkets in the Asian food section, whereas robust Koon Chun is mostly available at Chinese and Southeast Asian markets. Purchased hoisin is strong tasting, so thin it out with a bit of warm water before enjoying with a bowl of pho noodle soup.

Chile sauce contributes pleasant funky heat. Make a Viet-style chile sauce for pho (page 103), or buy sriracha. Thai brands like Sriraja Panich and Shark are closer in flavor to the kind used in Vietnam. Huy Fong's Rooster brand of sriracha is very strong and can obliterate the flavor of well-made pho if too much is used.

EQUIPMENT AND DISHWARE

Vietnamese cooking does not require loading up on fancy equipment. Depending on the pho soup recipe, you may need a **stockpot** to brew broth. Its tall shape facilitates gentle simmers and slow evaporation. If you must use a wide pot, partially cover it as the broth simmers to mitigate evaporation.

Your pho soup adventure will be easier with certain kitchen tools on hand. A **lightweight metal soup ladle** with a thin rim efficiently skims fat and pours broth into bowls. Before buying, hold it in your hand and mimic its use to determine if there's a good fit. A **noodle strainer** with a vertical handle is super for warming pho noodles and blanching bean sprouts in a deep saucepan of hot water. An **ultrafine mesh skimmer** constructed with silky smooth mesh makes scum removal a breeze. To efficiently strain broth, use a **medium or large mesh strainer** and **unbleached muslin** (see page 29). Shop at Asian markets, housewares stores, restaurant supply shops, and online for the strainers and skimmer. You won't regret having them.

The noodle soup recipes in this book yield moderate-size servings. For the **bowls**, I use 3½- to 4-cup (840 ml to 1 l) bowls about 7 inches (17.5 cm) in diameter. One with a flared lip is easier to carry to the table (use a tray or plate for an assist). You can always adjust the portion according to the bowls you own; my eclectic collection comes from travels to Vietnam, local artisans, Asian markets, and discount stores like Marshalls and Daiso. Once the noodles have been dunked and softened in hot water, they should occupy 20 to 25 percent of the bowl.

To eat the soup, use **chopsticks** and **Chinese soupspoons**. They're the traditional utensils for efficiently grabbing a bit of everything, but you may opt for forks and regular spoons. **Small dipping sauce dishes** are nice for hoisin, chile sauce, or saté sauce. Offer one for each person or several communal dishes to share.

NOODLE
STRAINER

MESH
SKIMMER

SOUP LADLE

TIPS, TRICKS, AND TECHNIQUES

Keep these insights in mind as you take your pho game to the next level.

Broth Basics

Pho broth contains the soup's essence. Here are some parameters and techniques for your knowledge base.

Understanding color and clarity is important to building good pho broth, which tends to be light and clear, not dark and dingy. The color is affected by the main ingredients, as well as by seasonings. Fish sauce darkens with a maple color. Dried shrimp lends an orange hue. Apple and napa cabbage inject a golden tinge. Clear broth comes from factors such as gentle cooking, parboiling bones, and straining. The starch on noodles naturally turns crystal-clear broth slightly cloudy. As long as the broth isn't mysteriously cloudy or looks like dishwater, it's fine.

Maintaining a gentle simmer slowly draws out flavors in broth that is made in a stockpot. Boiling clouds the broth and does not yield good flavor faster (try the quick pho and pressure cooker recipes if you're in a hurry). Bring the pot to a boil, then adjust the heat so that bubbles steadily percolate to the top, breaking the surface here and there. Occasionally check the simmering action and adjust the heat accordingly for moderate activity. Eyeball the water line to determine if the broth has cooked enough to achieve the recipe's broth yield. Remember, you can always simmer longer or add water to correct the broth.

Soaking cooked protein prevents meats from darkening and drying after they're pulled from the broth. Recipes often have you flush a whole chicken or pieces of chicken with tap water or soak chunks of beef in a bowl of water to cover. That quickly hydrates and cools the meat to prevent overcooking and an unappealing appearance. Follow instructions in the recipes for timing and approach. If you're in a hurry to chill down the meat for bowl assembly, use an ice bath, then refrigerate or perhaps freeze the meat. Bones saved for their marrow or tendon benefit from a soak, too.

Harvesting bits from bones is a resourceful way to add extra textural thrills. After the broth is done and the beef (or lamb) bones have cooled, pull or, if needed, scrape off sizable pieces of meat or chewable pieces of cartilage and tendon. Cool them in a bowl, cover, then chill. Cut them into bite-size pieces for bowl assembly.

Defatting broth is required for many pho recipes. After a broth is done, let it cool slightly and settle (see recipes for timing tips). The fat, which is less dense than water, will float at the top. Use a metal ladle to skim off some of the clear fat, depositing it into a small bowl or container.

Unless you're on a strict diet, leave large pools or a slick of fat behind; a fair amount of the spice notes lingers in the fat. If there's still too much fat in the broth after straining, let it settle and then reskim, or chill the broth and easily lift off the raft of solidified fat.

Saving pho fat creates a handy reserve of flavor for cooking and for seasoning the broth if it needs extra body or oomph. I use it in Pho Fried Rice (page 77), Panfried Pho Noodles (page 118), Deep-Fried Pho Noodles (page 120), and Pho Pot Stickers (page 129). If bits are suspended in the pho fat, strain it before using. If rogue broth remains in the fat, chill until solid, then separate the fat from the liquid. Don't waste the fat. Meat is precious, both fat and lean.

Straining broth can be done easily. After resting and defatting, remove large bones and bits that may disrupt the broth straining process. Position a mesh strainer over a pot (to gauge the pot size needed, double the recipe broth yield) and set both in the kitchen sink to work efficiently.

Line the strainer with a piece of lightweight unbleached muslin. Muslin catches impurities like a dream, is reusable, and costs less than cheesecloth; purchase it at a fabric store (ask for muslin suitable for lining quilts), tear it into squares about 18 inches (45 cm) wide, and wash before the first use.

Ladle in the broth or pick up the pot and carefully pour the broth through the strainer. As needed, lift the strainer to allow excess broth to flow through, or set the strainer on a measuring cup to catch residual broth.

After straining, rinse and then wash the muslin with fragrance-free soap to ensure a clean slate for the next batch. Without muslin, use a nut milk bag, or when in a pinch, try an ultrafine mesh skimmer, such as one used for skimming scum (see page 26).

Seasoning the broth happens in stages: as the broth brews and before using. To set savory-sweet base notes, the broth simmers with salt and perhaps Fuji apple, Chinese yellow rock sugar, or dried seafood. Close to bowl assembly time, the final seasoning happens. That's because broth can change as it sits, and fish sauce and other umami seasonings are somewhat volatile and their character fades over time.

Do the second seasoning when the broth is warm or hot, not boiling, to prevent a burnt tongue. Add the umami condiment for an "mmm . . . good" savory depth. The broth color naturally darkens from these condiments, but try not to darken it too much. If you need extra savoriness, add salt by the large pinch or ¼ teaspoon; see page 23 for salt equivalents.

Taste the broth. If it seems slightly off or rough on your tongue, achieve a savory-sweet finish with a touch of extra sweetness: maple syrup, organic cane sugar, or Chinese yellow rock sugar. At this point, traditional Viet cooks would also season with MSG or mushroom powder (see page 23) to create more umami depth. A spoon of reserved pho fat (see left) will inject extra body and spice notes. Right before ladling the broth into bowls, check it one last time and make any flavor tweaks.

Aim for a salty sweetness that's intense, a little stronger than you're comfortable with. Remember that the noodles, meats, and other elements in the pho bowl are either unsalted or lightly salted. The broth is what seasons them.

SODIUM IN PHO

"There's that much salt in there?" a friend once asked as I added salt to the broth. Yes, there is. Salt and fish sauce (or soy sauce or another salty liquid seasoning) are part of the umami foundation of pho. Because much of pho's flavor is conveyed by the broth, it needs to finish on the salty side. Don't be shy.

If you want low-sodium pho, back off the fish sauce in the final seasoning of the broth; a flavor enhancer could pick up the slack. Or, just follow the recipe and use less broth for each bowl. You'll serve more people.

Unusual Broth Techniques

Long-simmered old-fashioned pho cooked in a stockpot involves techniques that often confound cooks, but there are good reasons for them.

Charring ginger and onions (or shallots) seems fussy. Why bother with it? On a visceral level, the aroma of the burning onion, shallot, and ginger skin evokes open-flame cooking in Vietnam. On a practical level, this signature step in making pho *slightly* cooks the aromatics and converts their sugars. The pungency and heat remain to create the backbone flavor of pho. Viet cooks may have been trying to mimic the French method of roasting aromatics in an oven, but without proper ovens, they used charcoal braziers instead.

Modern cooks may use medium heat on a gas or electric coil burner, medium-hot heat on an outdoor grill or barbecue, or the broil setting in an oven (have the rack in the top or second position). Regardless, let the skin get a little splotchy with black; use tongs to occasionally rotate the ginger and onion (or shallot) and to grab and discard any flyaway skin. When working indoors, turn on the exhaust fan and open a window. To steady the aromatics on the stove, use a small grilling rack, heavy-duty broiling rack, or oven-safe cooling rack.

Monitor the aromatics because they char at different rates due to their uneven size and shape. After 10 to 15 minutes, they'll have softened slightly and become sweetly fragrant. Bubbling at the root or stem ends may happen. You do not have to blacken the entire surface. Remove from the heat and let cool for about 10 minutes.

Remove the charred skin from the cooled onions or shallots, and as needed, rinse under running water to dislodge stubborn dark bits. Trim off and discard the blackened root and stem ends; halve or quarter each and set aside.

Use a vegetable peeler or the edge of a teaspoon to remove the ginger skin. Rinse under warm water to remove blackened bits. Halve the ginger lengthwise, cut into chunks, then bruise lightly (use the broad side of a knife or a meat mallet). Set aside to add to the stockpot.

When shopping, select firm, solid onions or shallots. If using shallots, big ones endure the charring best. Choose ginger that's relatively straight; side knobs and little branches make it harder to char and peel. To avoid feeling rushed, char and peel the aromatics a day in advance and refrigerate; cut and bruise before using.

Parboiling bones is fabulous for efficiently producing clear, tasty broth. Valuable flavors are not lost when the bones are parboiled because it's done quickly with a minimal amount of water. What is rinsed off is lots of unwanted scum.

How to parboil the bones? Put them in the stockpot and add just enough water to *barely* cover. (Why waste water and energy?) Partially cover and bring to a boil over high heat. Uncover and let boil vigorously for 2 to 3 minutes to release the foamy impurities (think weird stuff at the beach).

Make sure the sink is clean and clear; if lots of small bones are involved, set a colander in the sink to catch them. Dump the parts and water into the sink and then rinse off any residue with water; a sprayer is extra helpful. Quickly scrub the stockpot clean and return the parts to the pot. Continue with the recipe.

Bowl Assembly Prep

It's fine to prep the various elements for the bowls close to serving, but some things may be readied ahead.

Noodles that work well for pho soup are narrow rice noodles the width of linguine or fettuccine (see page 19 for a buying guide); they may be dried or fresh. Some cooks boil dried pho noodles all the way through before assembling the bowls, but I prefer rehydrating them in water, then finishing their cooking via a dunk in boiling water. That approach allows dried noodles to function like fresh ones, which also require a brief dunk.

If dunking portions of soaked noodles seems like a chore, try my mom's approach: Boil medium-width pho noodles until cooked, then drain and set aside until assembly time. Divide the noodles among the bowls, add the cooked meat topping, and warm each bowl in the microwave oven (use 30-second blasts on medium-high). Finish with the remaining toppings (such as raw beef) and garnishes. Mom's method frees up a burner but the noodles may overcook. Cooked rice noodles often break once chilled, so use up what you've boiled.

When preparing **dried noodles** for recipes in this book, soak them in a bowl of hot tap water to cover until they are opaque and pliable, 10 to 30 minutes. The soaking time depends on the water temperature and the width and thickness of the noodles; Asian market noodles are usually thicker than supermarket varieties. Drain, rinse off excess starch, and then set aside to drain well. Use within 2 hours or store in a zipper plastic bag for up to 5 days.

There's a little more finesse involved when preparing **fresh noodles**. With the narrow ones sold in plastic bags, untangle the very long skein, snip with scissors into forearm lengths, and then set aside. If the noodles were sold on a Styrofoam tray, do your best to pry the strands apart; small bundles of noodles will later separate during dunking. To facilitate prying, you may warm and loosen the noodles in the microwave oven in 30-second blasts on medium-high.

Proteins for pho bowls should be prepped as bite-size pieces not only to stretch precious resources but also to make them retrievable with chopsticks and ensure that they get heated by the hot broth. For beef and lamb pho, it's easier to make thin cuts if the meat is firm and/or cold. That's why the meat is simmered to a firm doneness (make a fist and press the flesh at the base of your thumb to imagine the texture). If you can, chill or freeze it to further firm up. Slicing the raw steak (page 94) involves refrigeration. Pho shops often use deli meat slicers but a sharp knife works fine.

Chicken can be cut chilled or at room temperature since you're aiming for pieces of medium thickness; you may tear the flesh, too. Angle your knife to cut the Pan-Seared Tofu (page 97) into thin, broad pieces; the Pho Tempeh (page 99) is already cut in bite-size pieces. As needed, cut seitan and other mock meats into smallish pieces.

Garnishes such as onion, green onion, and cilantro may be prepped several hours in advance, kept in small bowls covered by plastic wrap, and refrigerated. If you don't like red or yellow onion, use additional green onion; unused green onion white parts may be poached in broth during bowl assembly and added to a few lucky bowls. Once the feathery tops of the cilantro sprigs have been chopped, save leftover stems for a chicken pho (pages 40, 46, and 59) or a pot sticker filling (pages 129 and 131). Ready condiments, garnish plates, and the like and set them at the table before you put together individual bowls. Herbs wilt if left out for hours, but condiments will be fine.

Pho Bowl Assembly

Have all of the components ready to go. The "quick pho" recipes on pages 40 to 45 call for dunking the noodles directly in the hot broth—a great shortcut for quickly serving two people, but the noodles will cloud the broth with their starch. When you've made pho from scratch, take a little extra time to set up and assemble the bowls like a pho professional. Your pho will taste better.

If you have friends assisting, one may dunk noodles, another may add toppings and garnishes, you may ladle broth, and someone else may deliver each bowl to the table; two nimble cooks can split the responsibilities, too. I often invite guests to assemble their own bowls. Regardless, the process is described below.

Reheat the broth to warm or hot, season it (see page 29 for tips), then lower the heat and cover to keep hot. At the same time, ready a deep saucepan filled with boiling water for blanching the noodles. Meanwhile, find a noodle strainer or mesh sieve to efficiently dunk noodles and/or vegetables in the pot of water. Have the proteins nearby, along with the onion, green onion, cilantro, and pepper.

To assemble each bowl, immerse a portion of the noodles into the pot of boiling (or near-boiling) water; wiggle with chopsticks (or a fork) or shake the strainer handle. When the noodles are sufficiently soft and hot (5 to 60 seconds; fresh, narrow noodles are ready in a flash), lift the strainer and give it a shake to force excess water back into the pot.

Dump the noodles into a bowl. Poke and wiggle with the strainer or chopsticks to flatten them out. Arrange the protein (and vegetables, if applicable) *flat* on top so that they'll be efficiently heated by the hot broth later on. Crown with the onion, green onion, and cilantro. Sprinkle on the pepper, if using.

Whether you're in a fluid assembly line with lots of people pitching in or just cooking alone, before dispensing the broth, retaste it and make last-minute tweaks if needed. Then return the broth to a boil and ladle into each bowl: Pour in a *circular pattern* to effectively heat things up. Bring to the table on a plate or tray if the bowl is too hot to carry with your fingers. Eat pho immediately.

Serving Pho Over Days

Depending on the recipe and your schedule, you may brew pho on one day and serve it the next, or enjoy it over the course of days. For example, make a batch during the weekend and prep a package of dried pho noodles (or have fresh noodles in the fridge). Eat what you want: For each serving, heat 2 cups (480 ml) broth and season with about 1½ teaspoons fish sauce, adding pinches of salt and sugar or maple syrup by the ¼ teaspoon. Refrigerate leftovers and repeat when it's pho time.

With the broth, noodles, and protein at hand, you can make a bowl in as little as 15 minutes. Pho broth and cooked proteins keep well for a good 3 days in the fridge; they can be frozen for 3 months.

Freezing Broth and Cooked Meats

For easy storage and thawing, fill zipper plastic bags with broth. Initially freeze them on trays or baking sheets so they'll freeze flat. To use, partially thaw to loosen the broth from the bag, then tap the bag on the edge of the counter or sink to break into pieces that will slide out into a pot for reheating. Wash, dry, and reuse the bag. Freeze uncut pieces of cooked meat separately. The broth and meat make a great frozen pho kit.

Wielding chopsticks in one hand and a Chinese soupspoon in the other, stir up the soup to distribute the flavors and agitate the noodles, which often get compacted during the assembly process. Then, taste and adjust the flavors with condiments and/or garnishes.

- Add bean sprouts, either raw for crunch or blanched first for a softer texture.

- Dip and wiggle thin slices of hot chile in the broth to release their heat and aroma. Leave them in longer if you dare.

- Strip fresh herb leaves from their stems, tear up large leaves, and drop them into your bowl. Set the stems on the table or a refuse dish.

- A sprinkle of Garlic Vinegar (page 106) brightens without overwhelming. A squeeze of lime lends a tart edge, which is especially nice if the broth is too sweet or bland. Set the spent lime wedge on the table or a refuse dish.

- If greater savory depth is needed, a sprinkle of fish sauce will remedy the situation.

- Many people squirt hoisin and chile sauce directly into their bowls, but a well-prepared broth suffers from such additions. Instead, make a yin-yang mixture in a small dish for dipping pieces of meat or a meatball. You'll pick up the condiment flavors without having them take over the broth.

- Slurp to show the cook your appreciation.

MARROW

NECK

KNUCKLE

FOOT

BEEF PHO TIPS

Options abound when you're selecting ingredients for beef pho. Here are tips to build the flavors and textures that you want.

Blending Bones

Beef pho broth made from all marrowbones is superb but quality beef bones can cost a lot, given that they're prized by other cooks and pet owners. As a work-around, blend the bones in a 1:1:1 ratio of marrow with affordable knuckle and neck bones, which, respectively, lend fat, body, and meatiness. Or try a 2:1 marrow to knuckle (or neck bones).

Some cooks tout oxtail, a pricey option that often dampens flavor and yields dull broth lacking dimension. For richness, select knuckle bones with connective tissue attached; harvest the tendon after cooking as a bonus. You can also add a pig's foot as suggested in the Hanoi-Style Beef Pho recipe on page 65, or 1 pound (450 g) of bone-in or boneless beef shank (keep it in the pot for 2 to 3 hours and use for the bowls and other dishes).

Sourcing and Selecting Bones

Ideal beef bones for pho are cut about 3 inches (7.5 cm) long. Look for them at supermarkets, ethnic grocers, natural foods markets, butcher shops, and farmers' markets. Beef leg bones (marrow and knuckle) may be labeled "soup bones" or "femur bones" at supermarkets and sold in bags at Chinese and Vietnamese markets. If the bones are huge, simmer longer and add water, as needed, to extract flavor.

Butchers who divide large sections of beef carcasses into small retail cuts likely have bones from grass-fed or naturally raised cows, which yield marvelous broth. Freeze bones from butchering other cuts for your pho. Neck bones may be sold fresh or frozen, normally at Asian and Latin markets and old-fashioned butchers.

Buying Beef Cuts

Select a husky chunk that will stay intact during cooking and be easy to thinly slice; a piece with some fat included is great for flavor. With the raw steak, also choose a hunky piece for sumptuous yet thin pieces.

For the boneless beef simmered in the broth, brisket yields marvelous, rich savor, followed by chuck and cross-rib roast. Rump is too lean and flavorless. For varied textures and mild chew, add shank as suggested in the discussion on blending bones.

Some people enjoy chewier drop flank (also called outside or rough flank), usually on pho menus as *nạm* and well done flank. Not the same as flank steak, the rectangular cut is comprised of a thin layer of flesh sandwiched between thick membranes. Sold at Chinese and Viet markets, it's displayed as vertical rolls. Buy about 1 pound (450 g), halve it crosswise, roll and tie each piece (try your best since it's naturally loose), then simmer in the broth for the entire 3 hours. Thinly slice to use.

Delicately crunchy book tripe (*sách*) is often precooked at Asian markets. Buy a piece the size of your hand, rinse, gently squeeze dry, then thinly slice into fringelike pieces to add during bowl assembly. Relatively exotic *vè dòn* (crunchy flank or skirt flank on menus) is best left to pho restaurants which have access to it. Adding pizzle to the bowl does not increase potency. Pho is a modest, humble affair. Plenty of delicious thrills can be had from readily available ingredients.

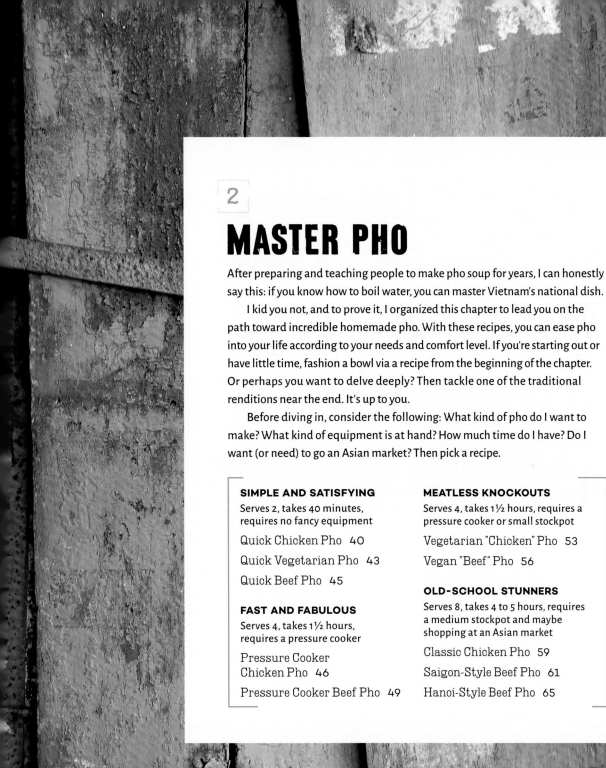

2

MASTER PHO

After preparing and teaching people to make pho soup for years, I can honestly say this: if you know how to boil water, you can master Vietnam's national dish.

I kid you not, and to prove it, I organized this chapter to lead you on the path toward incredible homemade pho. With these recipes, you can ease pho into your life according to your needs and comfort level. If you're starting out or have little time, fashion a bowl via a recipe from the beginning of the chapter. Or perhaps you want to delve deeply? Then tackle one of the traditional renditions near the end. It's up to you.

Before diving in, consider the following: What kind of pho do I want to make? What kind of equipment is at hand? How much time do I have? Do I want (or need) to go an Asian market? Then pick a recipe.

phở gà nhanh
QUICK CHICKEN PHO

Serves 2

Takes about 40 minutes

Great for pho beginners, this recipe is also terrific for cooks in a hurry. It involves less than 45 minutes, during which you'll doctor up store-bought broth so it says, "I'm pho-ish."

The keys to this streamlined approach include toasting spices and dry sautéing the ginger and green onion, which help to extract flavor fast. Poaching the chicken in the broth adds savory depth. You'll practice some fundamental pho techniques that you can apply elsewhere, too. Choose a broth that tastes like chicken, such as Swanson brand, which is less fussed up and easy to manipulate. You need two 14.5-ounce (411 g) cans or one 32-ounce (907 ml) carton.

¾-inch (2 cm) section ginger

2 medium-large green onions

1 very small (.5 oz | 15 g) bunch cilantro sprigs

1½ teaspoons coriander seeds

1 whole clove

3½ to 4 cups (840 ml to 1 l) low-sodium chicken broth

2 cups (480 ml) water

1 (6 to 8 oz | 180 to 225 g) boneless, skinless chicken breast or thigh

About ½ teaspoon fine sea salt

5 ounces (150 g) dried narrow flat rice noodles (see page 19)

2 to 3 teaspoons fish sauce

About ½ teaspoon organic sugar, or 1 teaspoon maple syrup (optional)

Pepper (optional)

Optional extras: Garnish Plate for 2 (page 100), ⅓ cup (90 ml) Ginger Dipping Sauce (page 107)

Peel then slice the ginger into 4 or 5 coins. Smack with the flat side of a knife or meat mallet; set aside. Thinly slice the green parts of the green onion to yield 2 to 3 tablespoons; set aside for garnish. Cut the leftover sections into pinkie-finger lengths, bruise, then add to the ginger.

Coarsely chop the leafy tops of the cilantro to yield 2 tablespoons; set aside for garnish. Set the remaining cilantro sprigs aside.

In a 3- to 4-quart (3 to 4 l) pot, toast the coriander seeds and clove over medium heat until fragrant, 1 to 2 minutes. Add the ginger and green onion sections. Stir for about 30 seconds, until aromatic. Slide the pot off heat, wait 15 seconds or so to briefly cool, then pour in the broth.

Return the pot to the burner, then add the water, cilantro sprigs, chicken, and salt. Bring to a boil over high heat, then lower the heat to gently simmer for 30 minutes.

While the broth simmers, soak the rice noodles in hot water until pliable and opaque. Drain, rinse, and set aside. (See page 32 for guidance.)

After 5 to 10 minutes of simmering, the chicken should be firm and cooked through (press on it and it should slightly yield). Transfer the chicken to a bowl, flush with cold water to arrest the cooking, then drain. Let cool, then cut or shred into bite-size pieces. Cover loosely to prevent drying.

When the broth is done, pour it through a fine-mesh strainer positioned over a 2-quart (2 l) pot; line the strainer with muslin for superclear broth. Discard the solids. You should have about 4 cups (1 l). Season with fish sauce and sugar (or maple syrup), if needed, to create a strong savory-sweet note.

Bring the strained broth to a boil over high heat. Put the noodles in a noodle strainer or mesh sieve and dunk in the hot broth to heat and soften, 5 to 60 seconds. Lift the noodles from the pot and divide between the 2 bowls.

Lower the heat to keep the broth hot while you arrange the chicken on top of the noodles and garnish with the chopped green onion, cilantro, and a sprinkling of pepper. Taste and adjust the broth's saltiness one last time. Return the broth to a boil and ladle into the bowls. Enjoy with any extras, if you like.

phở chay nhanh
QUICK VEGETARIAN PHO

Serves 2

Takes about 40 minutes

One of the secrets to making good and fast vegetarian pho is selecting the right broth at the store. Purchase an amber brown and robust broth, such as those made by Whole Foods or Swanson, which tends to be on the clear side and seasoned with spices that are more in line with pho; use two cans or one large carton. Avoid golden-hued vegetarian broths that are often celery forward and mute pho spices.

This pho does not cleverly fake beef or chicken pho like the ones on pages 53 and 56, but it echoes the seasonings and satisfying spirit of a good bowl of pho noodle soup. The mushrooms add meatiness, the tofu lends protein, and the quickly cooked green vegetables inject color and flavor. To make things easier for yourself at pho assembly time, make the seared tofu in advance.

¾-inch (2 cm) section ginger

2 medium-large green onions

1 star anise (8 robust points total)

1½ inches (3.75 cm) cinnamon stick

1 or 2 whole cloves

3½ to 4 cups (840 ml to 1 l) low-sodium or regular vegetable broth

2 cups (480 ml) water

About ½ teaspoon fine sea salt

5 ounces (150 g) dried narrow flat rice noodles (see page 19)

4 pieces Pan-Seared Tofu (page 97)

8 snap peas or slender green beans

2 or 3 fresh shiitake, king trumpet, or similar kind of meaty mushroom

2 to 3 teaspoons regular soy sauce

About ½ teaspoon organic sugar, or 1 teaspoon maple syrup (optional)

2 tablespoons chopped fresh cilantro, leafy tops only

Pepper (optional)

Optional extras: Garnish Plate for 2, Homemade Hoisin, Chile Sauce, Saté Sauce, Garlic Vinegar (pages 100 to 106)

Peel then slice the ginger into 4 or 5 coins. Smack with the flat side of a knife or meat mallet; set aside. Thinly slice the green parts of the green onion to yield 2 to 3 tablespoons; set aside for garnish. Cut the leftover sections into pinkie-finger lengths, bruise, then add to the ginger.

In a 3- to 4-quart (3 to 4 l) pot, toast the star anise, cinnamon, and cloves over medium heat until fragrant, 1 to 2 minutes. Add the ginger and green onion sections. Stir for about 30 seconds, until aromatic. Slide the pot off heat, wait 15 seconds to slightly cool, then pour in the vegetable broth. Return the pot to the burner, then add the water and salt. Bring to a boil over high heat, then lower the heat to gently simmer for 30 minutes.

While the broth simmers, soak the rice noodles in hot water until pliable and opaque. Drain, rinse, and set aside. (See page 32 for guidance.)

Prepare the tofu. (If you made the tofu in advance, let it warm up to room temperature.) Cut each finished tofu slab into thin slices or two large triangles. Set aside.

Cut the snap peas in half lengthwise; or cut the green beans into short lengths. Slice the mushrooms about ¼ inch (6 mm) thick. Set aside to later poach.

When the broth is done, pour it through a fine-mesh strainer positioned over a 2-quart (2 l) pot; line the strainer with muslin for superclear broth. Discard the solids. You should have about 4 cups (1 l). Season with soy sauce for a strong salty flavor; if needed, add sugar (or maple syrup) to refine edges.

continued

Bring the strained broth to a boil over medium-high heat. Put the noodles in a noodle strainer or mesh sieve and dunk in the hot broth to heat and soften, 5 to 60 seconds. Lift the noodles from the pot and divide between the 2 bowls. Repeat the dunking with the peas (or beans) and mushrooms to lightly poach in the broth, 30 to 60 seconds, depending on the vegetable; divide between the bowls.

Lower the heat on the broth to keep it hot while you add the tofu (if needed, warm it in the broth first), chopped green onion, cilantro, and sprinkling of pepper to the bowls.

Taste and adjust the broth's saltiness to your liking one last time. Return the broth to a boil, ladle into the bowls, and serve. Enjoy with any extras, if you like.

WARM BOWLS FOR HOT PHO

If it's cold in your home or your pho isn't hot enough, give the bowls a kiss of warmth before you fill them. Put the bowls in the oven, set it to the lowest temperature, about 170°F (75°C), and after it reaches temperature (about 15 minutes), turn off the oven as the bowls should be warm. If it's available, you can also use the oven's bread "proof" setting.

Alternatively, pour just-boiled water into a bowl, swish it around, then pour the water into an empty bowl and repeat. It's akin to warming teacups. Avoid making the bowls too hot because you'll be handling them during pho assembly.

phở bò nhanh
QUICK BEEF PHO

Serves 2

—

Takes about 40 minutes

When a fast beef pho is in order, try this recipe. It's similar to the chicken version on page 40, except the spices are bolder since beef pho can handle them. To let pho aromatics and spices shine, mix beef and chicken broth. The combination creates a lighter, appropriate canvas for painting a pho profile. Broths that taste like beef or chicken and not much else work best.

Thinly sliced roast beef sold at deli counters is fabulously convenient, and because it's minimally seasoned, it plays well with the pho flavors. Leftover cooked steak is terrific, too.

¾-inch (2 cm) section ginger

2 medium-large green onions

1 star anise (8 robust points total)

1½ inches (3.75 cm) cinnamon stick

1 or 2 whole cloves

1¾ to 2 cups (420 to 480 ml) low-sodium beef broth

1¾ to 2 cups (420 to 480 ml) low-sodium chicken broth

2 cups (480 ml) water

About ½ teaspoon fine sea salt

5 ounces (150 g) dried narrow flat rice noodles (see page 19)

4 to 5 ounces (115 to 150 g) very thinly sliced roast beef or cooked steak

2 to 3 teaspoons fish sauce

About ½ teaspoon organic sugar, or 1 teaspoon maple syrup (optional)

2 tablespoons chopped fresh cilantro, leafy tops only

Pepper (optional)

Optional Extras: Garnish Plate for 2, Homemade Hoisin, Chile Sauce, Saté Sauce, Garlic Vinegar (pages 100 to 106)

Peel then slice the ginger into 4 or 5 coins. Smack with the flat side of a knife or meat mallet; set aside. Thinly slice the green parts of the green onion to yield 2 to 3 tablespoons; set aside for garnish. Cut the leftover sections into pinkie-finger lengths, bruise, then add to the ginger.

In a 3- to 4-quart (3 to 4 l) pot, toast the star anise, cinnamon, and cloves over medium heat until fragrant, 1 to 2 minutes. Add the ginger and green onion sections. Stir for 30 seconds, until aromatic. Slide the pot off heat, wait about 15 seconds to cool a bit, then pour in the beef and chicken broths. Return

the pot to the burner, then add the water and salt. Bring to a boil over high, then lower the heat to gently simmer for 30 minutes.

While the broth simmers, soak the rice noodles in hot water until pliable and opaque. Drain, rinse, and set aside. (See page 32 for guidance.) Bring the beef to room temperature.

When the broth is done, pour it through a fine-mesh strainer positioned over a 2-quart (2 l) pot; line the strainer with muslin for superclear broth. Discard the solids. You should have about 4 cups (1 l). Season with fish sauce and sugar (or maple syrup), if needed, to create a strong savory-sweet note.

Bring the strained broth to a boil over high heat. Put the noodles in a noodle strainer or mesh sieve and dunk in the hot broth to heat and soften, 5 to 60 seconds. Lift the noodles from the pot and divide between the 2 bowls. Lower the heat to keep the broth hot while you arrange the beef on top of the noodles and garnish with the chopped green onion, cilantro, and a sprinkling of black pepper.

Taste and adjust the broth's saltiness to your liking one last time. Return the broth to a boil and ladle into the bowls. Enjoy with any extras, if you like.

Notes To take a shortcut for rare steak pho, buy about 5 ounces (150 g) of thinly sliced beef carne asada. Pound the meat a few times with a meat mallet to thin out further, then cut it into bite-size pieces for a quick pho topping.

phở gà nấu nồi áp suất
PRESSURE COOKER CHICKEN PHO

Serves 4

———

Takes about 1 hour, plus 30 minutes to cool

I grew up on old-fashioned pho that my mom simmered on the stove for hours. The house smelled great and the taste was fabulous. Alas, not everyone has that kind of time to make pho, so I developed this from-scratch method using the pressure cooker and ingredients sold at regular supermarkets and natural foods grocers.

It produces very good results in little time. I could call this the 15-minute pho, but that would overlook the time it takes to achieve high pressure, naturally cool the cooker, and complete other crucial steps. Plan on investing about 1½ hours to yield weekend-level pho to feed four people. You'll have leftover chicken for Chicken and Pho Fat Rice (page 81), Rice Paper Salad Rolls (page 135), or Spicy Chicken Slaw (page 142). A stockpot method is in Notes.

BROTH

1 (4 lb | 1.8 kg) whole chicken

1 rounded tablespoon coriander seeds

3 whole cloves

Chubby 2-inch (5 cm) section ginger, peeled, thickly sliced, and bruised

1 large (10 oz | 300 g) yellow onion, halved and thickly sliced

8 cups (2 l) water

1 small (4 oz | 115 g) Fuji apple, peeled, cored, and cut into thumbnail-size chunks

¾ cup (.7 oz | 20 g) coarsely chopped cilantro sprigs

2¼ teaspoons fine sea salt

About 1½ tablespoons fish sauce

About 1 teaspoon organic sugar, or 2 teaspoons maple syrup (optional)

BOWLS

10 ounces (300 g) dried narrow flat rice noodles (see page 19)

About half the cooked chicken from the broth

½ small (2 oz | 60 g) yellow or red onion, thinly sliced against the grain and soaked in water for 10 minutes

2 thinly sliced green onions, green parts only

¼ cup (.2 oz | 5 g) chopped fresh cilantro, leafy tops only

Pepper (optional)

Optional extras: Garnish Plate for 4 (page 100), Ginger Dipping Sauce (page 107)

Make the broth Rinse the chicken and set aside to drain. Put the coriander seeds and cloves in a 6- to 8-quart (6 to 8 l) pressure cooker. Over medium heat, toast for several minutes, shaking or stirring, until fragrant. Add the ginger and onion. Stir until aromatic, 45 to 60 seconds, to coax out a bit of flavor. A little browning is okay.

Add 4 cups (1 l) of the water to arrest the cooking process. Put the chicken in the cooker, breast side up. Add the apple, cilantro, salt, and remaining 4 cups (1 l) water. Lock the lid in place.

Bring to low pressure (8 psi) over high heat on a gas or induction stove, or medium heat on an electric stove. Lower the heat to maintain pressure, signaled by a gentle, steady flow of steam coming out of the cooker's valve. Cook for 15 minutes, or a few minutes longer if your cooker's low setting is less than 8 psi. If your cooker *only* has a high-pressure (15 psi) setting, cook for 12 minutes. Regardless, aim to gently poach the bird to yield silky cooked flesh.

When done, slide to a cool burner and let the pressure decrease naturally, about 20 minutes. Remove the lid, tilting it away from you to avoid the hot steam.

Let settle for 5 minutes before using tongs to transfer the chicken to a bowl; if parts fall off in transit, don't worry. Add water to cover the chicken and soak for 10 minutes to cool and prevent drying. Pour off the water, partially cover, and set the chicken aside to cool.

Skim some fat from the broth before straining it through a muslin-lined mesh strainer positioned over a medium pot (see page 28 for guidance). Discard the solids. You should have about 8 cups (2 l).

If using right away, season the broth with the fish sauce, extra salt, and perhaps the sugar (or maple syrup); see page 29 for broth seasoning tips. Or, partially cover the unseasoned broth and let cool, then refrigerate for up to 3 days or freeze for up to 3 months; reheat and season before using.

Use a knife to remove the breast halves and legs from the chicken. Set aside half of the chicken for another use. Reserve the remaining chicken for pho bowl assembly. The chicken can be refrigerated for up to 3 days or frozen for up to 3 months; bring to room temperature to use.

Prep and assemble the bowls While the broth cooks, or about 30 minutes before serving, ready the ingredients for the bowls. Soak the noodles in hot tap water until pliable and opaque. Drain, rinse, and drain well. (See noodle prep tips on page 32 for guidance.) Divide among 4 soup bowls.

Cut or tear the chicken breast and leg into pieces about ¼ inch (6 mm) thick. Discard the skin or save it for cracklings (see the Spicy Chicken Slaw recipe Notes, page 142). Place the onion, green onion, and cilantro in separate bowls and line them up with the noodles, chicken, and pepper for a pho assembly line.

Bring the broth to a simmer over medium heat as you are assembling the bowls. At the same time, fill a pot with water and bring to a rolling boil for the noodles.

For each bowl, use a noodle strainer or mesh sieve to dunk a portion of the noodles in the boiling water. When the noodles are soft, 5 to 60 seconds, pull the strainer from the water, shaking it to drain excess water back into the pot. Empty the noodles into a bowl. Top with chicken, then garnish with onion, green onion, cilantro, and pepper.

Check the broth flavor once more, raise the heat, and bring it to a boil. Ladle about 2 cups (480 ml) broth into each bowl. Enjoy immediately with any extras, if you like.

Notes To make this recipe in a 6- to 8-quart (6 to 8 l) stockpot, toast the coriander seeds and cloves over medium heat, then lightly cook the onion and ginger in the pot. Add 10 cups (2.5 l) water along with the chicken (breast up), cilantro, and salt. Partially cover, then bring to a boil over high heat. Uncover, skim the scum, then lower the heat to gently simmer, uncovered, for 2 hours. At the 45-minute mark, if the chicken is not cooking through, use tongs to rotate it. The chicken should be cooked after simmering for 1 to 1¼ hours. Transfer it to a large bowl, flush it with cold water, drain well, then set aside for 15 to 20 minutes to cool. When the broth is done, let rest for 15 minutes, then defat, strain, and season. The rest of the recipe is the same.

PHO FOR KIDS

Pho is deliberately served hot to ensure that all of the components are warmed and copacetic. That may challenge young diners. When a bowl is too hot to handle, drop a small ice cube into the child's bowl to quickly lower the temperature. You may also start kids out with cereal-bowl-size portions of noodles, toppings, and broth, or perhaps only noodles and broth.

phở bò nấu nồi áp suất
PRESSURE COOKER BEEF PHO

Serves 4
—
Takes about
1 hour, plus
30 minutes
to cool

As much as I love to simmer a stockpot of beef pho for hours, it's incredibly liberating to make a pretty good version for four people in 1½ hours. Intense cooking in a pressure cooker makes that possible. The approach is similar to that for the chicken version on page 46, but here, it's all high pressure.

The boneless meat gets a lot more tender than when cooked in a stockpot, which makes this beef a little harder to thinly slice (chill or freeze it, if you have time). Any leftover cooked beef can be used for Fresh Pho Noodle Rolls (page 133), Pho Fried Rice (page 77), or Rice Paper Salad Rolls (page 135). If you plan to make pho with all rare beef, or need the broth for other dishes such as Wok-Kissed Beef Pho (page 71), use ground beef instead of a boneless cut; details are in Notes.

BROTH

3 pounds (1.35 kg) beef marrow, knuckle, and neck bones (see page 37 for bone blending)

1 pound (450 g) boneless beef brisket, chuck, or cross-rib roast

2½ star anise (20 robust points total)

1 medium (3 in | 7.5 cm) cinnamon stick

3 whole cloves

Chubby 2-inch (5 cm) section ginger, peeled, thickly sliced, and bruised

1 large (10 oz | 300 g) yellow onion, halved and thickly sliced

9 cups (2.25 l) water

1 small (4 oz | 115 g) Fuji apple, peeled, cored, and cut into thumbnail-size chunks

2¼ teaspoons fine sea salt

About 2 tablespoons fish sauce

About 1 teaspoon organic sugar, or 2 teaspoons maple syrup (optional)

BOWLS

10 ounces (300 g) dried narrow flat rice noodles (see page 19)

Cooked beef from the broth, sliced about ⅛ inch (3 mm) thick

Thinly Sliced Steak (page 94) for 4 servings, 8 Beef Meatballs (page 95), or some of each (optional)

½ small (2 oz | 60 g) yellow or red onion, thinly sliced against the grain and soaked in water for 10 minutes

2 thinly sliced green onions, green parts only

¼ cup (.2 oz | 5 g) chopped fresh cilantro, leafy tops only

Pepper (optional)

Optional extras: Garnish Plate for 4, Homemade Hoisin, Chile Sauce, Saté Sauce, Garlic Vinegar (pages 100 to 106)

Make the broth Rinse the bones and boneless beef to remove excess blood or bits on the surface; set aside in a bowl.

Put the star anise, cinnamon, and cloves in a 6- to 8-quart (6 to 8 l) pressure cooker. Over medium heat, toast for several minutes, shaking or stirring, until fragrant. Add the ginger and onion. Stir until aromatic, 45 to 60 seconds, to release a little flavor. A tiny bit of browning is okay.

Add 4 cups (1 l) of the water to arrest the cooking process. Add all of the bones, boneless beef, apple, salt, and remaining 5 cups (1.25 l) water. Lock the lid in place. Bring to high pressure (15 psi) over high heat on a gas or induction stove, or medium heat on an electric stove. Lower the heat to maintain pressure, indicated by a gentle, steady flow of steam coming out of the cooker's valve. Cook for 20 minutes, or longer if your cooker's high setting is less than 15 psi.

Slide to a cool burner and allow the pressure to decrease naturally, about 20 minutes. Remove the lid, tilting it away from you to avoid the hot steam.

Let settle for about 5 minutes, then use tongs to transfer the boneless meat to a bowl. Add water to cover and soak for 10 minutes to prevent dark, dry meat (see page 28). Drain and set the meat aside, partially covered, to cool completely before using, refrigerating for up to 3 days, or freezing for up to 3 months.

continued

If you want to save bones for pho broth and bones (page 70) or to salvage edible bits, soak them in water for 10 minutes, then drain, prep, and store accordingly. Otherwise, discard the solids.

Skim some fat from the broth, then strain through a muslin-lined mesh strainer positioned over a medium pot (see page 28 for guidance). Discard the remaining solids. You should have about 8 cups (2 l).

If using the broth right away, season it with the fish sauce, extra salt, and, if needed, sugar (or maple syrup); seasoning tips are on page 29. Or, partially cover the unseasoned broth, let cool, then chill for up to 3 days or freeze for up to 3 months; reheat and season before using.

Prep and assemble the bowls While the broth cooks, or about 30 minutes before serving, ready the ingredients for the bowls. Soak the noodles in hot water until pliable and opaque. Drain, rinse, and drain well. (See noodle prep tips on page 32.) Divide among 4 soup bowls.

Slice the cooked beef, then prep the steak and/or meatballs, if using, as directed in their recipes. Set aside, covering the meat if not using in 15 minutes. Place the onion, green onion, and cilantro in separate bowls and line them up with the noodles, beef, and pepper for a pho assembly line.

Bring the broth to a simmer over medium heat as you are assembling the bowls. At the same time, fill a pot with water and bring to a rolling boil for the noodles.

For each bowl, place a portion of the noodles in a noodle strainer or mesh sieve and dunk in the boiling water. When the noodles are soft, 5 to 60 seconds, lift the strainer from the water, shaking it to force excess water back into the pot. Deposit into a bowl. Top with the beef, then add a flourish of onion, green onion, and cilantro. Sprinkle on some pepper.

Check the broth flavor once more, raise the heat, and bring it to a boil. Ladle about 2 cups (480 ml) broth into each bowl. Serve immediately with any extras at the table.

Notes Instead of boneless beef, use 1 pound (450 g) ground chuck. Simply break it up into chunks and add them to the cooker along with the bones.

To make this pho in a 6- to 8-quart (6 to 8 l) stockpot, toast the spices and dry sauté the aromatics as directed. Add 12 cups (3 l) water with the bones, boneless meat, apple, and salt. Partially cover and bring to a boil over high heat. Skim off the scum. Lower the heat to simmer, uncovered, for 3 hours. Midway, remove the boneless meat and soak in water to cool. When the broth is done, let rest for 15 minutes, then defat, strain, and season for assembly.

PRESSURE COOKER MODEL VARIATIONS

Writing recipes for appliances is difficult because of variations in makes and models. The pressure cooker recipes in this book were tested using stove-top models by Fagor and Kuhn Rikon and an electric Instant Pot. Cookers function differently, so when in doubt, check the pounds per square inch (psi) pressure level in your owner's manual (or look online) and hedge by slightly undercooking. You can always replace the lid and cook longer, or keep uncovered to boil off excess liquid. Make the recipe work with your cooker.

DIY PHO ROUTES: PRESSURE COOKER VERSUS STOCKPOT

It took me years to wrap my head around using a pressure cooker to make pho. I initially halved my stockpot pho recipes for the cooker and got incredibly viscous broth that was unfortunately blah. It didn't scream, "I am pho!" and I swore off pressure cooker pho. I considered slow cookers but pho is not a "set it and forget it" dish. Employing that appliance entails parboiling the bones for a clear broth and removing proteins partway through the simmering. It wasn't a game-changing approach.

Writing this book forced me to rethink pressure cooker pho. I wanted an intermediate level, time-saving method that appealed to busy cooks. Ingredients needed to come from supermarkets and mainstream grocers, which explains the Fuji apple for sweetness and ground beef option. The cooker intensely renders and melds flavors, so I slightly upped the spices, dumped charring the aromatics, and cut back on water and cooking time. The results were remarkably good and clear. I got hooked on making pressure cooker pho and pondered omitting the stockpot recipe altogether. My non-Viet husband protested and demanded a side-by-side taste test.

Which came out ahead? Both have their merits and you should decide based on your mood and situation. Cookers save time and natural resources, but the result represents 85 to 90 percent of what pho can be. It's pretty darn good but not outstanding. When I want a big batch of brilliant pho, or want to take an experimental pho to the next level, I use the traditional methods on pages 59 to 65. Otherwise, I grab the pressure cooker, put in the ingredients, and lock on the lid.

	MODERN PRESSURE COOKER	OLD-FASHIONED STOCKPOT
TIME REQUIRED	1½ hours	4 to 5 hours
RESOURCES	Uses less water and energy	Uses more water and energy
YIELD	4 bowls	8 bowls
FLAVOR AND TEXTURE	Emphasizes pho's gusto through deep flavors and rounder, heavier mouthfeel	Emphasizes pho's subtleties through lively flavors and delicate, nuanced mouthfeel
FAT	Clean separation of fat, so leave or return fat for flavor	Some fat suspended in the broth to capture pho essences
BROTH CLARITY	Clear with impurities separating and settling at the bottom	Clear with parboiling of bones
SPICES	Toasted for rapid extraction	Not toasted because the long simmer extracts flavor well
TREATMENT OF GINGER AND ONION	Dry sautéing instead of charring; the cooker's intensity voids the charred aromatics' nuances	Charring; adds layers of sweet heat and pungency and is one of the keys to creating traditional pho flavor
TARGET AUDIENCE	Great for cooks who want to get toes wet in DIY pho, make pho from scratch fast, experiment with new pho recipes	Best for cooks who want to observe the pho-making process, craft excellent pho, practice traditional pho techniques

phở gà chay
VEGETARIAN "CHICKEN" PHO

Serves 4

―――

Takes about
1 hour, plus
30 minutes
to cool

Whether you're a vegetarian, flexitarian, or omnivore, this and the following faux-meat pho recipes are worth trying. They are fun to make and delicious to eat.

The seasonings used here are the same as those employed for regular chicken pho. Celery adds a slightly earthy note while napa cabbage and carrot yield a golden-colored broth; the vegetables add natural juices so less water is needed. Yellow-colored nutritional yeast, sold at natural foods stores in the bulk section or spice section, lends a chicken-like umami flavor; it turns the broth cloudy naturally so I dissolve it in hot water, let it settle, then harvest the liquid portion for pho.

If vegetarian chicken substitutes (see page 55) are not for you, make the Pan-Seared Tofu or Pho Tempeh instead. You can also add half a boiled egg to each bowl, if you like (see egg instructions in Rotisserie Chicken Pho, page 82). A stockpot method is in Notes.

BROTH

1 whole clove

1 brimming teaspoon coriander seeds

Chubby 1-inch (2.5 cm) section ginger, peeled, thickly sliced, and bruised

1 medium-large (9 oz | 270 g) yellow onion, halved and thickly sliced

7 cups (1.75 l) cold water

1 small (4 oz | 115 g) Fuji apple, peeled, cored, and cut into thumbnail-size chunks

2 medium celery stalks (4 oz | 115 g total), coarsely chopped

1 large (6 oz | 180 g) carrot, cut into thick rounds (scrub and use unpeeled, if you like)

1 pound (450 g) napa cabbage leaves, halved lengthwise then cut crosswise into large pieces

1 cup (.9 oz | 25 g) coarsely chopped cilantro sprigs

2 teaspoons fine sea salt, plus more as needed

2½ tablespoons nutritional yeast powder, or 3½ tablespoons nutritional yeast flakes (.5 oz | 15 g total)

⅔ cup (150 ml) hot water

About 1 teaspoon organic sugar, or 2 teaspoons maple syrup (optional)

BOWLS

10 ounces (300 g) dried narrow flat rice noodles (see page 19)

8 to 10 ounces (225 to 300 g) vegetarian "chicken" substitute, Pan-Seared Tofu (page 97), Pho Tempeh (page 99), or some of each

½ small (2 oz | 60 g) yellow or red onion, thinly sliced against the grain and soaked in water for 10 minutes

2 thinly sliced green onions, green parts only

¼ cup (.2 oz | 5 g) chopped fresh cilantro, leafy tops only

Pepper (optional)

Optional extras: Garnish Plate for 4 (page 100), Chile Sauce (page 103), Saté Sauce (page 105), Garlic Vinegar (page 106)

Make the broth Put the clove and coriander seeds in a 6- to 8-quart (6 to 8 l) pressure cooker. Over medium heat, toast the spices for several minutes, shaking or stirring, until fragrant. Add the ginger and onion. Stir until aromatic, 45 to 60 seconds. A tinge of brown is okay.

Add 4 cups (1 l) of the cold water to arrest the cooking process. Add the apple, celery, carrot, cabbage, cilantro, salt, and the remaining 3 cups (720 ml) cold water. Lock the lid in place. Bring to high pressure (15 psi) over high heat on a

continued

gas or induction stove, or medium heat on an electric stove. Adjust the heat to maintain pressure, signaled by a gentle, steady flow of steam coming out of the cooker's valve. Cook for 15 minutes, or slightly longer if your cooker's high setting is less than 15 psi.

Meanwhile, in a small liquid measuring cup, combine the nutritional yeast with the hot water. Let sit about 10 minutes, until separated into two layers. Carefully pour the yellow liquid into a bowl and set aside. Discard the khaki sludge.

When the broth is done, slide the cooker to a cool burner and allow the pressure to decrease naturally, about 20 minutes. Remove the lid, tilting it away from you for safety. Let rest for 5 minutes, then strain through a muslin-lined mesh strainer positioned over a pot (see page 28 for guidance); briefly cool, then twist and press the muslin to yield more broth. Discard the solids. You should have about 8 cups (2 l) total.

To use right away, season the broth with the nutritional yeast liquid, sugar (or maple syrup), and up to ½ teaspoon extra salt. Aim for a savory-sweet, somewhat chicken-like flavor; warming the proteins in the broth later on will add depth, so go light on the saltiness here. (If cooking in advance, partially cover the unseasoned broth, let cool, then refrigerate for up to 3 days or freeze for up to 3 months. Prep the nutritional yeast and season the broth before using.)

Prep and assemble the bowls While the broth cooks, or about 30 minutes before serving, ready the ingredients for the bowls. Soak dried noodles in hot water until pliable and opaque. Drain, rinse, and drain well. (Noodle prep tips are on page 32.) Divide among 4 soup bowls.

Let the vegetarian "chicken" or other preferred toppings warm to room temperature. Meanwhile, place the onion, green onion, and cilantro in separate bowls and line them up with the noodles and pepper for a pho assembly line.

Bring the broth to a simmer over medium heat. At the same time, fill a pot with water and bring to a rolling boil for the noodles.

If seasoning bits are visible on the vegetarian "chicken," rinse them off before simmering in the broth to reheat and refresh, 1 to 2 minutes. Cool briefly, slice thinly, and set aside. With the tofu, cut on the diagonal into large triangles or thinly slice it. The tempeh needs no slicing. Warm the tofu or tempeh in the broth, if needed, then set aside.

For each bowl, place a portion of the noodles in a noodle strainer or mesh sieve and dunk in the boiling water. When the noodles are soft, 5 to 60 seconds, pull the strainer from the pot, shake it to release excess water, then empty the noodles into a bowl. Top each bowl with the vegetarian "chicken," tofu, and/or tempeh. Crown with onion, green onion, and cilantro. Sprinkle on some pepper.

Check the broth flavor again, add extra seasonings as needed, raise the heat, and bring it to a boil. Ladle about 2 cups (480 ml) broth into each bowl. Serve immediately with any extras at the table.

Notes To make the broth without a pressure cooker, use a 6- to 8-quart (6 to 8 l)stockpot. Ready the same set of broth ingredients but increase the water to 9 cups (2.25 l) total. Toast the spices, sauté the aromatics, then add the water, produce, and salt. Partially cover and bring to a boil. Lower the heat to a simmer and cook, uncovered, for 1 hour to yield a golden-hued broth. Strain and season with the nutritional yeast liquid, sugar (or maple syrup), and salt. Prep and bowl assembly is the same as above.

Instead of, or in addition to, nutritional yeast, use mushroom seasoning granules (page 23) for extra umami goodness. Add 3 or 4 pieces of kombu (dried kelp), each about 3 by 2 inches (7.5 cm by 5 cm), to the simmering broth to inject more savory depth. Try these tweaks with this recipe or with the faux pho recipe on page 56.

BUYING TIPS FOR VEGETARIAN MEAT SUBSTITUTES

Vegetarian meat substitutes are a culinary trompe l'oeil (French for "deceive the eye") that's pretty good for the planet. When shopping at natural foods stores and supermarkets, look for products with minimal seasonings or with a separate sauce packet that you may omit. Such "naked" mimickers take on the broth flavors well. Gardein, Quorn, and Beyond Meat are good brands; scan the ingredient labels for potential allergens. Seitan strips and slices by WestSoy and Sweet Earth are great for beef-like substitutes.

Before using vegetarian "meat" for pho, quickly rinse it to remove any surface seasonings. Poaching or simmering in the broth will reheat and refresh the product, allowing it to express its meaty texture as well as exchange flavors with the broth.

phở bò chay
VEGAN "BEEF" PHO

Serves 4

—

**Takes about
1 hour, plus
30 minutes
to cool**

As more people swap plant for animal protein, meatless dishes like this pho are not only easier to prepare (seitan strips, tempeh, and tofu are supermarket regulars) but also socially acceptable (they are not a deprivation food or hippie alternative).

To arrive at a beef-like pho broth, combine sweet, earthy, and slightly minerally vegetables. Fresh, regular white button mushrooms impart depth without darkening the broth too much, whereas dried mushrooms, such as shiitake and porcini, create superdark broths that scream "I am mushroom!" instead of "I am pholike."

Bragg Liquid Aminos and Maggi Seasoning sauce deliver the necessary umami notes; soy sauce does not have as beefy an impact, but you could use it in a pinch. This and the preceding recipe (see photo of both, page 52) are perfect for cooks interested in meatless cooking and/or crafting fabulous faux pho. Enjoy them with Saté Sauce (page 105) for a lemongrass-and-chile kick.

BROTH

2 whole cloves

1½ inches (3.75 cm) cinnamon stick

2 star anise (16 robust points total)

Chubby 1-inch (2.5 cm) section ginger, peeled, thickly sliced, and bruised

1 medium-large (9 oz | 270 g) yellow onion, halved and thickly sliced

7 cups (1.75 l) water

1 small (4 oz | 115 g) Fuji apple, peeled, cored, and cut into thumbnail-size chunks

2 small celery stalks (3 oz | 90 g total), coarsely chopped

1 medium (4 oz | 115 g) carrot, cut into thick rounds (scrub and use unpeeled, if you like)

4 ounces (115 g) white button mushroom, stems included, coarsely chopped

10 ounces (300 g) napa cabbage leaves, halved lengthwise then cut crosswise into large pieces

8 ounces (225 g) bean sprouts

1½ teaspoons fine sea salt, plus more as needed

2 tablespoons Bragg Liquid Aminos, or 1½ tablespoons Maggi Seasoning sauce

About 1 teaspoon organic sugar, or 2 teaspoons maple syrup (optional)

BOWLS

10 ounces (300 g) dried narrow flat rice noodles (see page 19)

8 to 10 ounces (225 to 300 g) seitan "beef" strips or slices, Pan-Seared Tofu (page 97), Pho Tempeh (page 99), or some of each

½ small (2 oz | 60 g) yellow or red onion, thinly sliced against the grain and soaked in water for 10 minutes

2 thinly sliced green onions, green parts only

¼ cup (.2 oz | 5 g) chopped fresh cilantro, leafy tops only

Pepper (optional)

Optional extras: Garnish Plate for 4, Homemade Hoisin, Chile Sauce, Saté Sauce, Garlic Vinegar (pages 100 to 106)

Make the broth Put the cloves, cinnamon stick, and star anise in a 6- to 8-quart (6 to 8 l) pressure cooker. Over medium heat, toast the spices for several minutes, shaking or stirring, until fragrant. Add the ginger and onion. Stir until aromatic, 45 to 60 seconds. A little browning is fine.

Add 4 cups (1 l) of the water to arrest the cooking process. Add the apple, celery, carrot, mushroom, cabbage, bean sprouts, salt, and the remaining 3 cups (720 ml) water. Lock the lid in place. Bring to high pressure (15 psi) over high heat on a gas or induction stove, or medium heat on an electric stove. Lower the heat to maintain pressure, indicated by a gentle, steady flow of steam coming out of the cooker's valve. Cook for 15 minutes, or slightly longer if your cooker's high setting is less than 15 psi.

When done, slide the cooker to a cool burner and allow the pressure to decrease naturally, about 20 minutes. Remove the lid, tilting it away from you to avoid the hot steam. Let rest for about 5 minutes before straining through a muslin-lined mesh strainer positioned over a medium pot (see page 28 for guidance); briefly cool, then twist and press the muslin to yield more broth. Discard the solids. You should have about 8 cups (2 l) total.

If using right away, season with the Bragg Liquid Aminos and, if needed, extra salt and sugar (or maple syrup). Aim for a savory-sweet, slightly meaty flavor; warming the proteins in the broth later on will add depth, so back off on being superbold here. (When cooking in advance, partially cover the unseasoned broth, let cool, then chill for up to 3 days or freeze for up to 3 months. Season it before using.)

Prep and assemble the bowls While the broth cooks, or about 30 minutes before serving, ready ingredients for the bowls. Soak dried noodles in hot water until pliable and opaque. Drain, rinse, and drain again. (See noodle prep tips on page 32.) Divide among 4 soup bowls.

Let the seitan or other preferred toppings warm up to room temperature. Meanwhile, place the onion, green onion, and cilantro in separate bowls, and arrange them with the noodles and pepper for a pho assembly line.

Bring the broth to a simmer over medium heat. Meanwhile, fill a pot with water and bring to a rolling boil for the noodles.

Separate the seitan strips, drain, and rinse if they're coated with heavy seasonings. Use a noodle strainer or mesh sieve to reheat and refresh the seitan in the hot broth, 1 to 2 minutes. Cool briefly and slice as needed. If using the tofu, cut on the diagonal into large triangles or thinly slice it. The tempeh needs no slicing. Warm the tofu or tempeh in the broth, if needed, then set aside.

For each bowl, reuse the noodle strainer to dunk a portion of the noodles in the boiling water. When the noodles are soft, 5 to 60 seconds, pull the strainer from the water, let the water drain back into the pot, then deposit the noodles into a bowl. Top with the seitan, tofu, and/or tempeh. Garnish with onion, green onion, and cilantro. Finish with pepper.

Retaste the broth, add seasonings as desired, raise the heat, and bring it to a boil. Ladle about 2 cups (480 ml) into each bowl. Serve immediately with any extras at the table.

Notes When making this recipe in a 6- to 8-quart (6 to 8 l) stockpot, gather and ready the same set of broth ingredients. The difference is that you'll increase the water to 9 cups (2.25 l) total. Toast the cloves, cinnamon, and star anise; sauté the ginger and onion; then add the water, apple, vegetables, and salt. Partially cover and bring to a boil. Lower the heat to a simmer and cook, uncovered, for about 1 hour to yield a lightly salted broth. Strain and, before using, finish with the final seasoning. Prep and assemble the bowls just like above.

If time allows, add nuance to a stockpot version of any pressure cooker pho recipe in this book by charring the onion and ginger. Keep the skin on and follow directions on page 30. After peeling and prepping, add to the pot with the water (skip the dry sauté step).

phở gà
CLASSIC CHICKEN PHO

Serves 8

—

Takes about 1 hour, plus 2¾ hours to simmer and cool

Most people assume that pho is a beefy affair, but a chicken version has been around since the late 1930s. It's actually easier to make than beef pho: there are fewer ingredients involved and less finesse required for superlative results. Given that, chicken pho is great for learning traditional techniques, such as charring aromatics and hacking bones. Some cooks flavor chicken pho the same way as beef pho, but I prefer to imbue the broth with coriander seeds and cilantro to create the tonic-like qualities of my mom's pho and what I've sampled in Hanoi.

Use good-quality chicken. I favor air chilled and occasionally buy a bird with everything intact (omit the head if it seems creepy). When chicken backs aren't available, use other inexpensive parts, such as drumsticks. Freeze the backs and other parts when prepping chicken to make this delectable pot of Vietnamese chicken noodle soup. When buying the rock sugar at the Asian market, look for fresh pho noodles for an extra treat.

BROTH

Chubby 4-inch (10 cm) section ginger, unpeeled

1 pound (450 g) yellow onion, unpeeled

3 pounds (1.35 kg) chicken parts, such as backs, necks, wings, feet, and drumsticks

1 (4 lb | 1.8 kg) whole chicken, rinsed and patted dry

5 quarts (5 l) water

2 tablespoons coriander seeds

4 whole cloves

1 small bunch (1 oz | 30 g) cilantro

½ ounce (15 g) Chinese yellow rock sugar (see page 23)

1½ tablespoons fine sea salt

About 3 tablespoons fish sauce

BOWLS

1¼ pounds (565 g) dried narrow flat rice noodles, or 2 pounds (900 g) fresh pho noodles (see page 19)

Cooked chicken from the broth, cut or torn into bite-size pieces about ¼ inch (6 mm) thick

½ medium (3 oz | 90 g) yellow or red onion, thinly sliced against the grain and soaked in water for 10 minutes

3 or 4 thinly sliced green onions, green parts only

½ cup (.35 oz | 10 g) chopped fresh cilantro, leafy tops only

Pepper (optional)

Optional extras: Garnish Plate for 8 (page 100), Ginger Dipping Sauce (page 107)

Make the broth Char, peel, and prep the ginger and onion as instructed on page 30. Set aside.

Prep the chicken parts. Wield a heavy cleaver or knife suitable for chopping bones to whack the bones and parts: Break them partway or all the way through to expose the marrow, making the cuts at 1½-inch (3.75 cm) intervals. Work efficiently, with the flatter side of each part facing down. Direct the action from your wrist (not elbow). Imagine vanquishing a foe.

Switch attention to the whole chicken. Look in the body cavity for the neck, heart, gizzard, and liver. If included, add the neck (first give it a few whacks), heart, and gizzard to the parts bowl; the liver may dirty and impart an off flavor, so save it for something else.

Since wings tend to fall off during cooking, detach each one: bend it back (like a long arm stretch) and cut off at the shoulder/armpit joint. Whack each wing a few times and add to the parts bowl. Set the wingless bird aside.

To achieve a clear broth, parboil and rinse the chicken parts; see page 28 for guidance and use a medium stockpot, about 12-quart (12 l) capacity. After rinsing off the impurities, quickly scrub the pot, and return the parts to it. Add the

continued

wingless chicken, breast side up. Pour in the water and make sure the chicken is submerged. Partially cover and bring to a boil over high heat. Uncover and lower the heat to gently simmer.

Use a ladle or skimmer to remove scum that rises to the top. Add the ginger and onions, plus the coriander seeds, cloves, cilantro, rock sugar, and salt. Readjust the heat to gently simmer uncovered.

After 25 minutes, the wingless chicken should be cooked; its flesh should feel firm yet still yield a bit to the touch. Use tongs to grab and transfer the chicken to a large bowl. Flush it with cold water, drain well, then set aside for 15 to 20 minutes to cool. Meanwhile, keep the broth simmering.

When the chicken can be handled, use a knife to remove each breast half and the whole legs (thigh and drumstick). Don't cut these pieces further, or they'll lose their succulence. Set on a plate to cool completely, then cover, and refrigerate for up to 3 days or freeze for up to 3 months; bring to room temperature for bowl assembly.

Return the leftover carcass and remaining bony bits to the stockpot. Adjust the heat to gently simmer for 1½ hours longer. Total simmering time is roughly 2¼ hours, depending on the chicken's cooling time.

When done, let rest for 20 minutes to settle the impurities and further concentrate the flavor. Skim some fat from the broth, then use a slotted spoon to remove most of the bony parts, dumping them into a bowl for refuse. Strain the broth through a muslin-lined mesh strainer positioned over a large pot (see page 28 for guidance). Discard the solids. You should yield about 4 quarts (4 l).

If using the broth right away, season it with the fish sauce and extra salt (seasoning tips are on page 29). When making the broth ahead, partially cover the unseasoned broth, let cool, then refrigerate for up to 3 days or freeze for up to 3 months; reheat and season before using.

Prep and assemble the bowls About 30 minutes before serving, ready ingredients for the bowls. Soak dried noodles in hot water until pliable and opaque; drain, rinse, then let drain well. If using fresh noodles, untangle or separate them, and snip as needed. (See page 32 for noodle prep tips.) Divide them among 8 soup bowls.

Prep the chicken, discarding the skin, if you want. Set aside. Place the onion, green onion, and cilantro in separate bowls and line them up with the noodles and pepper for a pho assembly line.

Bring the broth to a simmer over medium heat. At the same time, fill a pot with water and bring to a rolling boil for the noodles.

For each bowl, place a portion of the noodles in a noodle strainer or mesh sieve and dunk in the boiling water. When the noodles are soft, 5 to 60 seconds, pull the strainer from the water, shaking it to let water drain back into the pot. Empty the noodles into a bowl. Top with chicken, then add the onion, green onion, and cilantro. Finish with pepper.

Taste and check the broth flavor again, adjust if desired, then raise the heat and bring it to boil. Ladle about 2 cups (480 ml) of broth into each bowl. Serve immediately with extras at the table.

Notes A fancied-up bowl of chicken pho may contain *trứng non*, which are mild-tasting, immature chicken eggs that are considered very special. There's no need to chase down such a rarity. Simply add half a boiled egg to each bowl. Instructions for boiling eggs are in the Rotisserie Chicken Pho recipe on page 82.

If you have a lemon or lime tree, pluck 2 or 3 tender leaves. Cut them into the finest, threadlike pieces (omit the spines) and add a pinch along with the cilantro. The leaf is an extra traditional touch.

phở bò sài gòn
SAIGON-STYLE BEEF PHO

Serves 8

—

Takes about 1 hour, plus 3½ hours to simmer and cool

Here's the beef pho that I grew up with. My mother brewed it from memories and flavors that spanned decades, as well as the Pacific Ocean. Born near Hanoi, Mom migrated to Saigon in 1954, where she met and married Dad, also a northerner. She adopted southern-style pho, which was slightly sweetened by rock sugar. She omitted medicinal black cardamom, which reminded her of the strident north. Then in America, she switched from using shallot (too pricey for our refugee family) to yellow onion, its natural sweetness lending complexity to the broth, its raw pungency adding edge to the bowl.

At home, she remained a northerner at heart, serving pho with only fresh chile and mint. At pho shops, I've spied her tucking Thai basil and bean sprouts into her bowl. She's grounded in tradition but open to change. I have modified my mom's recipe over the years and she uses mine today, adding her own touches. I hope you will too.

BROTH

Chubby 4-inch (10 cm) section ginger, unpeeled

1 pound (450 g) yellow onion, unpeeled

6 pounds (2.7 kg) beef marrow, knuckle, and neck bones (see page 37 for bone blending)

5½ quarts (5.5 l) water

5 star anise (40 robust points total)

6 whole cloves

1 husky (3 in | 7.5 cm) cinnamon stick

1½ pounds (675 g) boneless beef brisket, chuck, or cross-rib roast, cut into 2 pieces

½ ounce (15 g) Chinese yellow rock sugar (see page 23)

1½ tablespoons fine sea salt

About ¼ cup (60 ml) fish sauce

BOWLS

1¼ pounds (565 g) dried narrow flat rice noodles, or 2 pounds (900 g) fresh pho noodles (see page 19)

Cooked beef from the broth, sliced about ⅛ inch (3 mm) thick

Thinly Sliced Steak for 8 (page 94), 16 Beef Meatballs (page 95), or some of each (optional)

½ medium (3 oz | 90 g) yellow or red onion, thinly sliced against the grain and soaked in water for 10 minutes

3 or 4 thinly sliced green onions, green parts only

½ cup (.35 oz | 10 g) chopped fresh cilantro, leafy tops only

Pepper (optional)

Optional extras: Garnish Plate for 8, Homemade Hoisin, Chile Sauce, Saté Sauce (pages 100 to 105)

Make the broth Char, peel, and prep the ginger and onion as instructed on page 30. Set aside.

To achieve a clear broth, parboil and rinse the beef bones; see page 28 for guidance and use a medium stockpot, about 12-quart (12 l) capacity. After rinsing off the impurities and scrubbing the pot, return the bones to it.

Pour in the water, partially cover, then bring to a boil over high heat. Uncover and lower the heat to a gentle simmer. Use a ladle or skimmer to remove any scum that rises to the top. Add the charred ginger and onions, plus the star anise, cloves, cinnamon, boneless beef, rock sugar, and salt. Bring to a simmer, adjust the heat, and gently simmer, uncovered, for 3 hours.

At the 1½-hour mark, remove the boneless beef, which should feel firm (it will be easier to thinly slice later). Transfer to a bowl, add water to cover, and soak for 10 minutes to prevent dry, dark meat (see page 28). Drain and set the meat aside, partially covered, to cool completely before using, refrigerating for up to 3 days, or freezing for up to 3 months. Meanwhile, maintain the broth at a steady simmer for the remaining 1½ hours.

continued

When the broth is done, let rest for 20 minutes to settle the impurities and further concentrate the flavor. Use tongs to remove bones and any large, retrievable bits. To save the bones for pho broth and bones (page 70) or to salvage edible bits from them, soak the bones in water for 10 minutes, then drain, prep, and store accordingly. Otherwise, discard the solids.

Skim some fat from the broth, then strain it through a muslin-lined mesh strainer positioned over a large pot (guidance is on page 28). You should have about 4 quarts (4 l).

If using the broth right away, season it with the fish sauce and with extra salt and rock sugar (seasoning tips are on page 29). When cooking in advance, partially cover the unseasoned broth, let cool, then refrigerate for up to 3 days or freeze for up to 3 months; reheat and season before using.

Prep and assemble the bowls About 30 minutes before serving, ready ingredients for the bowls. Soak dried noodles in hot water until pliable and opaque; drain, rinse, then let drain well. If using fresh noodles, untangle or separate them and snip as needed. (Extra prep tips are on page 32.) Divide the noodles among 8 soup bowls.

Cut the cooked beef as directed. If using sliced steak and/or meatballs, prep them as directed in their recipes. Cover and set aside if not using in 15 minutes.

Place the onion, green onion, and cilantro in separate bowls. Line them up with the noodles, beef topping(s), and pepper for a pho assembly line. Set the broth on medium heat to reheat and bring a pot of water to a boil for the noodles.

For each bowl, place a portion of the noodles in a noodle strainer or mesh sieve and dunk in the boiling water. When the noodles are soft, 5 to 60 seconds, lift the strainer from the pot, shaking it to force excess water back into the pot. Empty the noodles into a bowl. Top with the cooked beef and any other beef topping. Shower on the onion, green onion, and cilantro. Finish with a sprinkle of pepper.

Check the broth flavor once more, then raise the heat to bring it to a boil. Ladle about 2 cups (480 ml) broth into each bowl. Serve immediately with any extras at the table.

CHINESE ROCK SUGAR SUBSTITUTE

If you don't want to use (or do not have) Chinese yellow rock sugar for the Saigon-Style Beef Pho here and Classic Chicken Pho on page 59, add Fuji apple and dried seafood. Use the quantities and instructions in the Hanoi-Style Beef Pho recipe on page 65.

Or prepare the broth with the apple only (use the same amount), and when doing the final seasoning with fish sauce and salt, round out the flavors with up to 2 teaspoons organic sugar or 4 teaspoons maple syrup; that's the same approach as for the pressure cooker pho recipes (page 46 to 57).

phở bắc
HANOI-STYLE BEEF PHO

Serves 8

—

Takes about 1 hour, plus 3½ hours to simmer and cool

If you know pho as bodacious, sweet-savory bowls served with a pile of vegetables and various condiments, you only know its southern Viet incarnation. Many pho aficionados argue that Hanoi-style, or northern, pho is the best and truest.

What are the differences? Northern pho broth is more savory than sweet, thanks to dried seafood like *sá sùng*, or peanut worms, available at markets such as Hanoi's Dong Xuan, but it's fine to substitute dried scallop, shrimp, and anchovies. The toppings usually only include cooked beef and/or raw beef, green onion, and cilantro. Accessories are few: garlic vinegar, sliced chile, and mint. For richness, people dip fried breadsticks into the broth.

I've been refining this recipe since 2010, picking up tricks from locals. Hanoi chefs insisted that shallots were better than yellow onion for their pho and they were right. My cousin Quyen included fresh sugarcane for sweetness; I answered with Fuji apple. Tracey Lister of the Hanoi Cooking Centre suggested a pig's foot for viscosity. When sliced steak isn't part of the bowl, simmer the full amount of beef to make sure you have enough. I grew up on Saigon-style pho but this recipe blows my mind every time. Make it to experience the subtle genius of pho.

BROTH

Chubby 4-inch (10 cm) section ginger, unpeeled

4 huge shallots (12 to 16 oz | 350 to 450 g total), unpeeled

6 pounds (2.7 kg) beef marrow, knuckle, and neck bones (see page 37 for bone blending)

1 pig's foot, a good 1 pound (450 g), precut by the butcher into 4 or 5 pieces (optional)

5½ quarts (5.5 l) water

1½ to 2 pounds (675 to 900 g) boneless beef brisket, chuck, or cross-rib roast, cut into 2 or 3 pieces

½ to ¾ ounce (15 to 25 g) dried scallop or dried shrimp (see Notes)

5 star anise (40 robust points total)

1 husky (3 in | 7.5 cm) cinnamon stick

1 very large Chinese black cardamom, crushed with a meat mallet to expose seeds

2 teaspoons fennel seeds

1½ tablespoons fine sea salt

1 medium (6 oz | 180 g) Fuji apple, peeled, cored, and cut into thumbnail-size chunks (optional)

About ¼ cup (60 ml) fish sauce

BOWLS

1¼ pounds (565 g) dried narrow flat rice noodles, or 2 pounds (900 g) fresh pho noodles (see page 19)

Cooked beef from the broth, sliced about ⅛ inch (3 mm) thick

Thinly Sliced Steak for 8 (page 94; optional)

6 slender or 4 medium green onions, white and green parts, cut on a sharp diagonal into long, thin pieces

½ cup (.35 oz | 10 g) chopped fresh cilantro, leafy tops only

Pepper (optional)

2 Fresno, Thai, or serrano chiles, thinly sliced

8 to 12 sprigs mint

Garlic Vinegar (page 106)

8 Fried Breadsticks (page 109; optional)

continued

Make the broth Char, peel, and prep the ginger and shallot as instructed on page 30. Set aside.

To achieve a clear broth, parboil and rinse the bones and pig's foot (if using). See page 28 for tips, and use a medium stockpot, about 12-quart (12 l) capacity. After rinsing off impurities and scrubbing the pot, return the bones (and foot) to it.

Pour in the water, partially cover, and bring to a boil over high heat. Uncover and lower the heat to a gentle simmer. Use a ladle or skimmer to remove scum that rises to the top. Add the charred ginger and shallot, plus the boneless beef, dried scallop (or shrimp), star anise, cinnamon, cardamom, fennel, salt, and apple (if using). Adjust the heat to maintain a simmer and cook, uncovered, for 3 hours.

At the 1½-hour mark, remove the boneless beef, which should feel very firm (it'll be easier to thinly slice). Transfer to a bowl, add water to cover, and soak for 10 minutes to prevent dark, dry meat (see page 28). Drain and set the meat aside, partially covered, to cool completely before using, refrigerating for up to 3 days, or freezing for up to 3 months. Meanwhile, maintain the broth at a steady simmer for the remaining 1½ hours.

When the broth is done, let rest for 20 minutes to settle the impurities and further concentrate the flavor. Use tongs to remove bones and any large, retrievable bits. To save bones for pho broth and bones (page 70) or to salvage edible bits from them, soak them in water for 10 minutes, then drain, prep, and store accordingly. Otherwise, discard the solids.

Skim some fat from the broth, then strain it through a muslin-lined mesh strainer positioned over a large pot (see page 28 for guidance). You should have about 4 quarts (4 l).

If using the broth right away, season it with the fish sauce and extra salt; broth seasoning tips are on page 29. Or, partially cover the unseasoned broth, let cool, then refrigerate for up to 3 days or freeze for up to 3 months; reheat and season before using.

Prep and assemble the bowls About 30 minutes before serving, ready ingredients for the bowls. Soak dried noodles in hot water until pliable and opaque; drain, rinse, then let drain well. If using fresh noodles, untangle or separate them and snip as needed. (See noodle prep tips on page 32.) Divide them among 8 soup bowls.

Slice the cooked beef as directed. Prep the sliced raw steak, if using. Set all of the beef aside, covering it if not using in 15 minutes.

Place the green onion and cilantro in separate bowls, then line them up with the noodles, beef topping(s), and pepper for a pho assembly line. Set the chiles, mint, and garlic vinegar at the table. If serving fried breadsticks, refresh them (if needed) according to their recipe. Bring the broth to a simmer over medium heat and bring a pot of water to a boil for the noodles.

For each bowl, place a portion of the noodles in a noodle strainer or mesh sieve and dunk in the boiling water. When the noodles are soft, 5 to 60 seconds, remove the strainer from the water, shaking it to let excess water drain back into the pot. Empty the noodles into a bowl. Top with the cooked beef and with the raw beef, if using. Add showers of green onion and cilantro. Finish with the pepper.

Do a final broth tasting, return it to a boil, then ladle about 2 cups (480 ml) into each bowl. Enjoy immediately with the extras at the table.

Notes Dried scallop and dried shrimp are loaded with umami to add alluring sweet-savory depth to pho broth and other dishes. Dried scallop has a refined flavor that works exceptionally well for the Hanoi-style pho. You may use more affordable dried shrimp, but the results fall just shy of brilliant. If you do opt for the shrimp, use the excess for Saté Sauce (page 105).

Both dried shrimp and scallop are sold in plastic packages in the refrigerated foods section at Chinese and Viet markets. Buy whole shrimp in size medium or large because they have more flavor than little ones. Small, more affordable dried scallops are what I keep on hand. Refrigerate or freeze the packages indefinitely. If an off-ammonia odor develops, it's time to restock.

When shellfish is an issue, substitute dried anchovies. They're used for certain Japanese and Korean soup stocks and have lots of umami. Buy the small fish (about the length of a pinkie finger) at an Asian market; they're called *iriko* and *niboshi* in Japanese and *mareum-myeolchi* in Korean. Use ¾ ounce (25 g). Snap off and discard the heads. Pinch each at the belly to open and use a fingertip to remove and discard the crumbly, bitter black guts. Toss into the pot as you would the shrimp or scallop.

If you acquire *sá sùng* (sea worms) from Vietnam, use ½ to ¾ ounce (15 to 25 g) and omit the dried scallop or shrimp. To remove sand inside the worms, toast them in a dry skillet over medium heat for 1 to 2 minutes, turning and shaking the skillet, until slightly inflated. Cool, then use scissors to cut each worm into short lengths. Pour out the sand and quickly rinse, if needed. Add to the broth with the ginger and shallot.

FINAL MASTER PHO SOUP TIP

Follow the recipes in this book to establish your pho skills, then confidently experiment. Pho has never been a static dish with only one recipe. Build on the foundation that I've given you here. Tweak the spice blend to suit your favorite flavors (see page 20 for pointers). Combine onion and shallot in the broth for subtle complexity.

Create a *đặc biệt* special combo pho by adding different cuts from a Chinese or Viet market, such as drop flank and boneless shank; see page 37 for more details. Assemble bowls with flavorful, snappy homemade meatballs (page 95). Enjoy pho with different herbs to witness the interaction of aroma and flavor. The Adventurous Pho chapter starting on page 69 offers recipes to propel you forward.

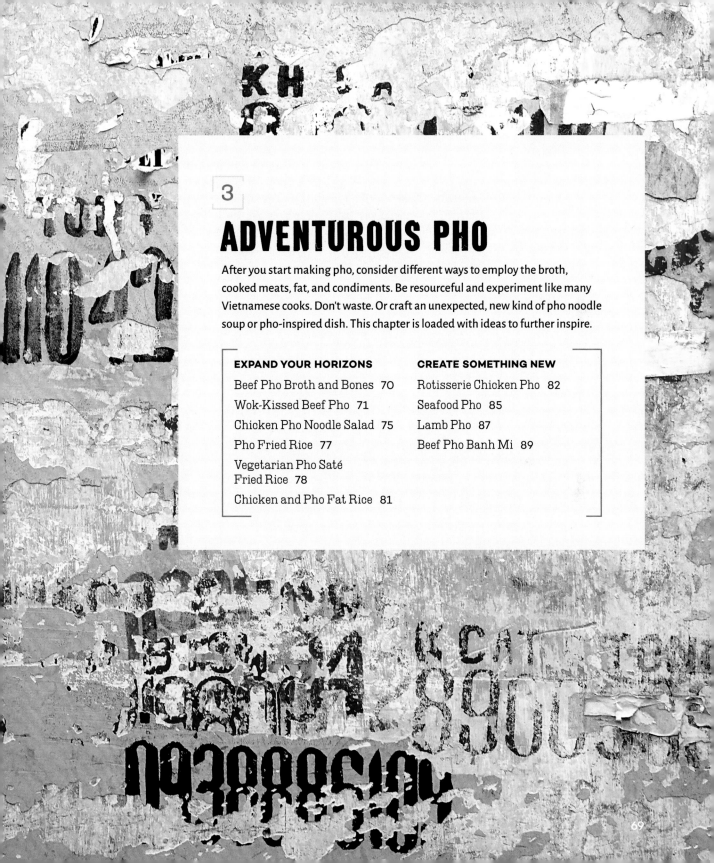

3

ADVENTUROUS PHO

After you start making pho, consider different ways to employ the broth, cooked meats, fat, and condiments. Be resourceful and experiment like many Vietnamese cooks. Don't waste. Or craft an unexpected, new kind of pho noodle soup or pho-inspired dish. This chapter is loaded with ideas to further inspire.

xáo xương bò
BEEF PHO BROTH AND BONES

Serves 4

—

Takes
20 minutes

At a Viet restaurant in Las Vegas, I ordered a dish called "The Big Bone Soup." The waitress delivered a serving bowl filled with pho broth and *Flintstones*-size beef bones left over from brewing the broth. Along with chopsticks and soupspoons, we were given forks and knives to retrieve the marrow and scrape off the edible bits clinging to the bones. A smart way to use up pho resources, the dish was primal and fun to eat, too.

At home, you may take a more elegant route for a starter course or light lunch. Offer handsome bones (gnarly ones may put off guests) and slices of the cooked beef along with broth and garnishes. Gild the lily with fried breadsticks or substitute baked crostini as suggested in Notes.

3 cups (720 ml) beef pho broth (any kind from Master Pho chapter, page 39)

Fish sauce

Fine sea salt

¼ small (1 oz | 30 g) red onion, thinly sliced against the grain

2 slender green onions, white and green parts, cut on a sharp diagonal into long, thin pieces

4 Fried Breadsticks (page 109)

3 or 4 sprigs cilantro, mint, and/or Thai basil

1 Fresno or jalapeño chile, thinly sliced, or 4 tiny Thai chiles, partially split lengthwise

1 lime, cut into wedges

Optional extras: Homemade Hoisin (page 102), Chile Sauce (page 103), Saté Sauce (page 105)

4 to 8 bones saved from the broth, at room temperature

12 to 16 slices cooked beef from the broth

Pepper (optional)

Select a pan that's large enough to hold the broth and all of the bones. Pour in the broth, then season with fish sauce and salt to taste. Aim for a pleasant savory flavor (instead of a bold one), since you're not adding noodles and other items. Heat over medium-low; lower the heat and cover if it comes to a boil.

Put the onion and green onion in a bowl, add water to cover, and soak for 10 minutes to reduce harshness. Drain and set aside. If needed, reheat the fried breadsticks

according to the recipe instructions; set at the table with the herbs, chile, lime, and any extra sauces.

Raise the heat to bring the broth to a near boil. Add the bones, and after a few minutes when they're hot and refreshed, use a slotted spoon to divide among 4 individual soup bowls or transfer to a serving bowl. Strew the sliced beef around the bones. Return the broth to a boil, then ladle into the bowl(s). Garnish with the onion, green onion, and pepper. Serve with the extras.

Invite guests to use the knife to push and dislodge the marrow and carve off tendon and other bits from the bones. Dip the breadsticks into the broth and spread marrow on them. Add garnishes, dip cooked beefy bits in condiments, and slurp on broth just like regular pho noodle soup.

Notes Don't want to fry breadsticks? Make crostini from a French-style baguette (what you'd use to prepare banh mi, for example). Preheat the oven to 375°F (190°C). Cut 12 to 16 slices, each about ⅓ inch (8 mm) thick. Arrange as one layer on a parchment paper–lined baking sheet. In a small saucepan, melt 2 tablespoons butter with 2 tablespoons neutral oil, such as canola. Brush onto the top side of each slice of bread. Bake for 15 to 20 minutes, until golden and crisp. Cool on a rack. Enjoy at any temperature.

phở áp chảo
WOK-KISSED BEEF PHO

Serves 4

———

Takes about 30 minutes

Beef pho is not always about cooked and/or rare meat. You can put a stir-fry in it to create this ridiculously good dish. Some cooks use a topping of beef and vegetables, but the flavors distract and dilute the broth too much. This recipe (also called *phở tái lăn*) is based on my mom's favorite, what she savored in Hai Duong, the northern Vietnamese city where was born and raised.

"*Áp* means to lightly touch," she explained, softly pressing her cheek to mine. "*Chảo* refers to a wok or skillet." Then she described the dish of her 1940s childhood: The street vendor briefly warmed fresh rice noodles in his hot wok to let it pick up a bit of *wok hei* essence and fatty richness. After emptying the noodles into a bowl, he quickly stir-fried beef, onion, and garlic and added them to the noodles. The broth was ladled into the bowl or served on the side, if the customer desired. It was simple and tasty, she recalled.

After learning that I created this recipe, she asked me to prepare it for her. Mom had frozen pho broth so it was supereasy to whip up. She wholeheartedly approved. Now you can try it yourself.

10 ounces (300 g) dried medium flat rice noodles, or 1 pound (450 g) fresh pho noodles (see page 19)

2 tablespoons plus 1 teaspoon canola or other neutral oil, plus more as needed

12 ounces (350 g) well-trimmed beef top sirloin or flank steak, cut across the grain into bite-size strips a scant ¼ inch (6 mm) thick

¼ teaspoon pepper, plus more as needed

¾ teaspoon sugar

1 teaspoon cornstarch

2 teaspoons fish sauce, plus more as needed

2 teaspoons regular soy sauce

8 cups (2 l) beef pho broth (see Notes)

Salt

2 cloves garlic, finely chopped

½ small (2 oz | 60 g) yellow or red onion, cut along the grain into narrow wedges

2 slender green onions, white and green parts, cut on a sharp diagonal into long, thin pieces

¼ cup (.2 oz | 5 g) chopped fresh cilantro, leafy tops only

Optional extras: Garnish Plate for 4 (page 100), Garlic Vinegar (page 106)

If using dry noodles, boil them in a pot of water for 5 to 7 minutes, until tender chewy (or use package directions, if available). Drain, rinse off lingering starch, then let sit to drain well. Toss with 1 teaspoon of the oil to prevent sticking and set aside. Fresh noodles are often already oiled; pry them apart and set aside.

Combine the beef in a bowl with the ¼ teaspoon pepper, sugar, cornstarch, fish sauce, and soy sauce. Set aside.

Reheat the pho broth in a small pot and season it with fish sauce and salt, as needed; if it comes to a boil, lower the heat and cover. Set the noodles and beef by the stove with the garlic, onion, green onion, and cilantro. Have the garnish plate and/or garlic vinegar at the table.

To cook, use a large, well-seasoned wok or nonstick skillet. Heat over medium to medium-high heat. Add a small splash of oil if you're worried about the noodles sticking. Add the noodles and stir-fry for about 1 minute, until they soften slightly and begin to stick together. Remove from the heat and divide among 4 noodle soup bowls.

As needed, wash and dry the wok (or skillet). Heat it over medium-high heat. Swirl in the remaining 2 tablespoons oil. Add the garlic and onion. Once aromatic, about 30 seconds, bank the aromatics on one side of the pan.

continued

Increase the heat to high and add the beef, spreading it out into a single layer. Let it cook, undisturbed, for about 1 minute. When the beef begins browning, use a spatula to flip and stir for 1 to 2 minutes, until it is still slightly rare.

Divide the beef among the bowls. Garnish with green onion and cilantro. Sprinkle on some pepper. Retaste the broth, make any adjustments, then bring to a boil and ladle into the bowls. Serve immediately with any extras. Invite guests to enjoy this like other pho noodle soup.

Notes Since you're not using the pho-cooked meat for this preparation, it may be conveniently prepared with the Quick Beef Pho broth (page 45) or the Pressure Cooker Beef Pho (page 49) using ground beef. The long-simmered stockpot pho broth (pages 61 and 65) would be welcomed, too. You can also experiment with lamb or chicken thigh, stir-frying it until done; pair the meat with the broth.

READ RECIPES AND PREP LIKE A PRO

For space efficiency, recipes written in American cookbooks present ingredients in order of usage, which is not necessarily the order of prep. Identify items that can or should be made in advance. Ingredients that will eventually be thrown into the pan together may be kept together (why dirty up extra dishes?). If fast-paced cooking is involved, such as stir-frying, line up the prepped ingredients by the stove and have needed equipment handy so you don't have to scramble at the end. When cooking multiple dishes, cluster the ingredients for each dish on the counter or a baking sheet to lessen confusion. You'll be ready to rock and roll.

phở gà trộn
CHICKEN PHO NOODLE SALAD

Serves 4 as a light main course

—

Takes about 30 minutes

You would think that Hanoi, the birthplace of Viet culture and pho, would stay close to tradition. But it's actually a city open to new pho ideas, such as this chicken and rice noodle salad dressed with a tangy-spicy soy sauce and served with a side of hot pho broth. The broth is enjoyed as a chaser to the somewhat intense noodles and chicken.

Pho Hanh on Lan Ong Street in the Old Quarter is one of the most popular spots for this dish. One balmy Saturday night when I was there, the sidewalk seating was packed with young families, friends, and couples. Pho Hanh used to specialize in traditional chicken pho but switched to the salad to offer a cooling version of pho soup in the warmer months. It's simply a good batch of chicken pho presented differently, which explains why it seems unusual yet tastes familiar.

Make this with leftover chicken and broth, or poach 1 pound (450 g) boneless chicken in the Quick Chicken Pho broth on page 40; there will be enough liquid for the sauce and broth side. The Notes section has ideas for variations.

4 cups (1 l) broth from Quick Chicken Pho (page 40), Pressure Cooker Chicken Pho (page 46), or Classic Chicken Pho (page 59)

½ teaspoon fine sea salt

2½ tablespoons sugar

1 tablespoon Chile Sauce (page 103) or sriracha sauce, plus more for serving

2 tablespoons unseasoned Japanese rice vinegar

3 tablespoons regular soy sauce

1½ tablespoons canola or other neutral oil

2 teaspoons finely chopped garlic, or rounded ¾ teaspoon Pho Spice Blend (page 111)

1½ teaspoons cornstarch, dissolved in 2 teaspoons water

10 ounces (300 g) dried medium flat rice noodles (see page 19)

Fish sauce

12 ounces (350 g) cooked chicken from any chicken pho recipe (see Chapter 2: Master Pho, page 39)

2 thinly sliced green onions, green part only

2 cups (2 oz | 60 g) butter lettuce or soft leaf lettuce, cut into narrow ribbons, with spines intact

¼ cup (.2 oz | 5 g) coarsely chopped fresh cilantro, leafy tops only

⅓ cup (.35 oz | 10 g) coarsely chopped fresh mint or Thai basil leaves

⅓ cup (1.4 oz | 40 g) unsalted, roasted peanuts, coarsely chopped

⅓ cup (about 1.3 oz | 35 g) fried shallots or onion, homemade or purchased

Combine ½ cup (120 ml) of the broth with the salt, sugar, chile sauce, vinegar, and soy sauce. Set this sauce mixture near the stove.

Put the oil and the garlic or spice blend in a small saucepan. Heat over medium-low heat until the garlic sizzles and is light blond (3 to 4 minutes), or the spice blend is lightly fragrant (1 minute). Move the pan off heat and wait about 15 seconds to cool slightly, then pour in the sauce mixture. Replace over high heat and bring to a boil. Stir the cornstarch, then swirl into the bubbly sauce. Once thickened, about 15 seconds, slide to a cool burner. Let rest for 10 minutes before using. You should have about 1 cup (240 ml).

Meanwhile, boil the noodles in a pot of water for 5 to 7 minutes, until tender chewy (if available, use package directions). Drain, cool quickly under running water, then set aside to drain and cool.

Taste the remaining broth (about 3½ cups | 840 ml) and season with fish sauce as needed to create a lovely savory finish. Reheat the broth in a saucepan over medium heat.

continued

Meanwhile, cut or shred the chicken into bite-size pieces and, if needed, warm in a microwave oven to remove the chill and refresh; ideally the chicken has some succulence. Set aside.

To assemble, have 4 rice bowls for broth and 4 noodle-soup-size bowls for the salad. Put a little green onion into each rice bowl (use the rest for the noodle salad). Set near the broth.

Divide the lettuce among the noodle soup bowls. Add a portion of noodles and chicken, then about ¼ cup (60 ml) of the sauce. Top with the remaining green onion, cilantro, mint (or basil), peanut, and fried shallots (or onion).

Ladle the hot broth into the rice bowls. Serve immediately with the noodle salad bowls. Invite guests to wield spoons and chopsticks to toss their salads and enjoy the broth as soothing interludes. If the noodles seem too heavy with sauce, mix in a spoonful of broth. Offer extra chile sauce to heat seekers.

Notes For a **vegetarian pho noodle salad**, employ the Vegetarian "Chicken" Pho broth (page 53) and Pan-Seared Tofu (page 97) or Pho Tempeh (page 99).

The sauce may be made 2 days in advance and refrigerated; return it to room temperature before using. The vegetables and noodles may be prepped hours in advance. If the noodles harden, soften them in the microwave oven via 30-second blasts. Ideally, they're warmish.

Instead of lettuce, substitute blanched bean sprouts and carrot. Use about 6 ounces (180 g) bean sprouts and 2 ounces (60 g) carrot, cut into matchstick-size strips. Blanch to tender-crisp in the pot set up for the noodles, then cook the noodles.

cơm chiên nước phở
PHO FRIED RICE

Serves 4 as a side dish

Takes about 45 minutes, plus 1 to 2 hours for cooling the rice

This recipe came to exist because I didn't want to waste a stash of pho fat. I began making fried rice, and the fat coated the grains with pho flavor. It was good, but cooking the rice in pho broth made it taste better. To reinforce the pho spirit and enliven things, I added pho spices and a flourish of fresh herbs and garlic vinegar at the table. The result was delicious.

To cook the rice, use any pho broth from this book. When possible, match the broth with the fat. Taste the broth and if it's too salty, add water; salty condiments are added during the frying phase. Gelatinous broth can yield unevenly cooked rice that's oddly gummy or hard in spots; to avoid that, dilute viscous broth via a 4:1 or 3:1 ratio of broth to water.

1 cup (6.5 oz | 195 g) raw long-grain rice, such as jasmine

1¼ cups (300 ml) mildly salty pho broth, any kind from Master Pho chapter (page 39), Rotisserie Chicken Pho (page 82), Seafood Pho (page 85), or Lamb Pho (page 87)

2 tablespoons pho fat, European-style butter, or canola or other neutral oil

1 clove garlic, finely chopped

½ medium (3 oz | 90 g) red or yellow onion, cut along the grain into narrow wedges

1 large egg, beaten

2 teaspoons fish sauce or regular soy sauce, plus more as needed

1 teaspoon Maggi Seasoning sauce or Bragg Liquid Aminos

½ to ¾ teaspoon Pho Spice Blend (page 111), or ¼ teaspoon pepper

1 medium green onion, white and green parts, chopped

Fine sea salt

Garlic Vinegar (page 106; optional)

2 or 3 bushy sprigs Thai basil or mint

Wash the rice well and drain in a mesh strainer. Dump the rice into a small saucepan. Add the broth and bring to a boil over high heat. Lower the heat slightly, give the rice a stir, and let bubble for a few minutes, stirring occasionally, until glossy on top. A few craters may form. Turn the heat to low, cover, and let cook for 10 minutes. Turn off the heat and let rest for 10 minutes. Uncover, fluff the rice with chopsticks or a fork, then rest again for 10 minutes to finish cooking. Turn the rice onto a small baking sheet, spreading it out. Let cool completely (1 to 2 hours), uncovered, before using; or cover and refrigerate overnight.

Before frying the rice, stir it up to prevent lumps. Set near the stove with the fat, garlic, onion, egg, fish sauce (or soy sauce), Maggi (or Bragg), spice blend (or pepper), green onion, and salt.

Heat a large, well-seasoned wok or nonstick skillet over high heat. Swirl in 1 tablespoon of the fat, then add the garlic and onion. Stir-fry for about 15 seconds, until aromatic. Add the rice and briskly stir-fry for about 2 minutes, until warm and slightly revived.

Push the rice to the perimeter to create a well in the middle. Add the remaining 1 tablespoon fat to the well. Pour in the egg. Pour the fish sauce and Maggi around the rim on the rice. Quickly stir-fry to cook the egg and work it into the rice. Add the spice blend and green onion. Cook for 10 to 15 seconds longer, until just wilted. Turn off the heat, taste, and add salt, if needed. Transfer to a plate or shallow bowl. Serve with the garlic vinegar, if using, and Thai basil. Invite guests to pluck, tear, and mix the herb leaves into the rice. They may sprinkle on and mix in the vinegar at will.

Notes For a shortcut, use 3 cups (15 oz | 425 g) day-old cooked rice. For extra protein, top the rice with a fried egg. Or, before adding the rice to the pan, add a handful of chopped tofu, crumbled tempeh, cooked meat, or seafood.

cơm chiên nước phở chay
VEGETARIAN PHO SATÉ FRIED RICE

Serves 4 as a side dish

—

Takes about 45 minutes, plus 1 to 2 hours for cooling the rice

The preceding pho fried rice begot this punchy vegetarian rendition. Eaters who eschew meat should not be left out of the pho scene. Because the vegetarian pho broths are lean, the saté sauce (prepare it in advance) is the perfect choice for adding fatty flavor. If you like, top the rice with a fried egg, and at the table, mix it in for richness. Omnivores will enjoy this fried rice, too, and of course, you can turn this recipe into something meaty by using regular saté sauce and switching out the pho broth and protein.

1 cup (6.5 oz | 195 g) raw long-grain rice, such as jasmine

1¼ cups (300 ml) broth from Quick Vegetarian Pho (page 43), Vegetarian "Chicken" Pho (page 53), or Vegan "Beef" Pho (page 56)

4 ounces (115 g) Pho Tempeh (page 99), or 4 pieces Pan-Seared Tofu (page 97)

2 tablespoons vegetarian Saté Sauce (see Notes on page 105)

1 clove garlic, finely chopped

2 medium green onions, white and green parts, chopped

Fine sea salt

2 or 3 bushy sprigs Thai basil or mint

Regular soy sauce, Maggi Seasoning sauce, or Bragg Liquid Aminos

Wash the rice well and drain in a mesh strainer. Dump the rice into a small saucepan. Add the broth and bring to a boil over high heat. Lower the heat slightly, give the rice a stir, and let bubble for a few minutes, stirring occasionally, until glossy on top. A few craters may form. Turn the heat to low, cover, and let cook for 10 minutes. Turn off the heat and let rest for 10 minutes. Uncover, fluff the rice with chopsticks or a fork, then let rest again for 10 minutes to finish cooking. Turn the rice onto a small baking sheet, spreading it out. Let cool completely (1 to 2 hours), uncovered, before using; or cover and refrigerate overnight.

Before frying the rice, stir it up to prevent lumps. Crumble the tempeh, or cut the tofu into cubes the size of large peas. Set by the stove with the saté sauce, garlic, green onion, and salt.

Heat a large, well-seasoned wok or nonstick skillet over high heat. Pour in the saté sauce, then add the garlic. Stir-fry for 5 to 10 seconds before adding the tempeh or tofu. Cook briskly for 30 to 45 seconds to combine well. Add the rice. Stir-fry for about 2 minutes longer, until heated through.

Add the green onion. Cook for 10 to 15 seconds longer, until just wilted. Turn off the heat, taste, and add salt, if needed. Transfer to a plate or shallow bowl. Present with the Thai basil (or mint) sprigs. Invite guests to pluck, tear, and mix the herb leaves into the rice. Sprinkle on the soy sauce (or other seasoning) for an umami boost, if needed.

Notes I wrote this and the Pho Fried Rice recipe (page 77) to be prepared with long-grain white rice, such as jasmine. If you prefer another kind of rice, adjust the broth amount accordingly. Aim for chewy-soft grains that separate nicely for fried rice. For example, I prepare "quick cooking" Thai brown jasmine rice produced by Three Ladies and Golden Star using about 1⅓ cups (330 ml) broth or water for 1 cup (6.5 oz | 195 g) raw rice. That approach differs from package instructions but works for me.

cơm gà
CHICKEN AND PHO FAT RICE

Serves 4 as a main course

Takes about 1 hour

I often have leftover chicken from a pot of pho, particularly the pressure cooker recipe on page 46. Taking a page from chicken pho restaurants, I use the meat and some of the broth and fat to make a flavorful chicken and rice. Lots of garlic and ginger get fried in the fat, resulting in a dish similar to Hainanese chicken and rice. However, I serve mine with a Viet ginger-lime dipping sauce as well as with soy sauce and chile. If two sauces are too much, just offer the gingery one.

If there's extra chicken pho broth around, serve it on the side. Add a light salad for a balanced meal. This is a rice lover's dream dish.

2 cups (13 oz | 390 g) raw long-grain rice, such as jasmine

2⅓ cups (570 ml) broth from Pressure Cooker Chicken Pho (page 46), or Classic Chicken Pho (page 59), or low-sodium chicken broth

Fish sauce

Fine sea salt

1 tablespoon finely chopped garlic

1 tablespoon peeled and finely chopped ginger

3 tablespoons chicken pho fat, canola oil, or a combination of both

½ cooked chicken (breast and leg) from Pressure Cooker Chicken Pho (page 46) or Classic Chicken Pho (page 59), at room temperature

⅔ cup (150 ml) Ginger Dipping Sauce (page 107)

2 tablespoons regular soy sauce

1 tablespoon water

4 or 5 Fresno or jalapeño chile slices

1 firm-ripe tomato, sliced

½ English cucumber or 1 Persian cucumber, cut into thin rounds or ovals

Wash the rice to remove some of its starch. Drain in a mesh strainer and set atop a bowl to dry for 10 minutes. Meanwhile, taste the broth and season with fish sauce and salt, if needed. Heat the broth in a saucepan until hot. If it comes to a boil, cover and lower the heat to keep hot.

Over medium heat in a 3- to 4-quart (3 to 4 l) pot, gently sauté the garlic and ginger in the fat until aromatic, about 1 minute. Add the rice and fry, stirring often, until opaque, about 3 minutes. Lower the heat slightly or pull off heat, then add all of the hot broth.

Replace the pot on the burner and raise the heat. Let boil vigorously, stirring frequently until little craters form. Lower the heat to low and cover. Cook for 10 minutes. Turn off the heat and let sit for 10 minutes to finish cooking. Fluff with chopsticks or a fork. Let rest 10 to 30 minutes before serving.

While the rice cooks, make the ginger dipping sauce and put in a small serving bowl. For the other sauce, combine the soy sauce, water, and chiles in a small bowl. Set both sauces at the table.

If needed, use the microwave oven to warm the chicken, 1 to 1½ minutes on medium or medium-high. Cut into bite-size pieces off the bone or, for a more authentic service, chop with a meat cleaver and leave on the bone.

Serve the chicken and rice along with the tomato and cucumber on individual dinner plates and enjoy with fork, knife, and spoon. Or, offer the rice in rice bowls and the chicken, tomato, and cucumber on a plate and wield chopsticks. Sauces should be on the side for guests to help themselves.

Notes Make the rice up to 3 days in advance and microwave to reheat. Little extra tweaks include garnishing the rice with crisp fried shallot or onion and offering sprigs of Vietnamese coriander (*rau răm*, included in the photo) on the side to add herbal notes. Try dipping the chicken in Viet-style Chile Sauce on page 103.

phở gà quay
ROTISSERIE CHICKEN PHO

Serves 4

**Takes about
45 minutes,
plus 1¼ hours
to simmer
and cool**

Pho was born from make-do cooking, and in that spirit, I use leftovers from a purchased rotisserie chicken to make this tasty soup. The carcass, unwanted bits, and lingering juices go into a stockpot with aromatics and vegetables to build and extend the chicken flavor. (Yes, there's a similarity to the Vegetarian "Chicken" Pho recipe on page 53.) I save some meat for the bowls, supplementing it with halved boiled eggs.

Weigh the carcass, especially if you love to clean every speck of meat off the bones. The broth is slightly cloudy from the carcass but it still has good flavor. See Notes for pressure cooker tips and day-after Thanksgiving turkey pho.

BROTH

1 pound (450 g) leftover roast chicken carcass, skin, and unwanted parts

1 small (4 oz | 115 g) Fuji apple, peeled, cored, and cut into thumbnail-size chunks

1 medium (2 oz | 60 g) celery stalk, coarsely chopped

1 small (3 oz | 90 g) carrot, cut into thick rounds (scrub and use unpeeled, if you like)

8 ounces (225 g) napa cabbage leaves, halved lengthwise then cut crosswise into large pieces

1 small bunch (1 oz | 30 g) cilantro, stems and leaves coarsely chopped

2 star anise (16 robust points total)

2 whole cloves

Brimming 1½ teaspoons coriander seeds

1½ inches (3.75 cm) cinnamon stick

Chubby 2-inch (5 cm) section ginger, peeled, cut into thick slices, and bruised

1 medium-large (9 oz | 270 g) yellow onion, halved and cut into thick slices

10 cups (2.5 l) water

1½ teaspoons fine sea salt, plus more as needed

About 1½ tablespoons fish sauce

About 1 teaspoon organic sugar, or 2 teaspoons maple syrup (optional)

BOWLS

10 ounces (300 g) dried narrow flat rice noodles, or 1 pound (450 g) fresh pho noodles (see page 19)

2 to 4 large eggs, at room temperature

6 to 8 ounces (180 to 225 g) rotisserie chicken meat, torn into pieces about ¼ inch (6 mm) thick

½ small (2 oz | 60 g) yellow or red onion, thinly sliced against the grain and soaked in water for 10 minutes

2 thinly sliced green onions, green parts only

¼ cup (.2 oz | 5 g) chopped fresh cilantro, leafy tops only

Pepper (optional)

Optional extras: Garnish Plate for 4, Homemade Hoisin, Chile Sauce, Saté Sauce (pages 100 to 105)

Make the broth Use your hands to break up the chicken carcass into chunky pieces so you can easily submerge them in liquid later. Set aside in a large bowl along with the apple, celery, carrot, cabbage, and cilantro. Keep near the stove.

Put the star anise, cloves, coriander seeds, and cinnamon in a small stockpot, about 8-quart (8 l) capacity. Over medium heat, toast the spices for several minutes, shaking or stirring, until fragrant. Add the ginger and onion and stir for 45 to 60 seconds, until lightly fragrant. Add 4 cups (1 l) of the water to arrest the cooking process. Add the carcass, apple, vegetables, salt, and the remaining 6 cups (1.5 l) water.

Partially cover and bring to a boil over high heat; there's usually little scum to skim. Uncover and lower the heat to lightly simmer for 1 hour. When done, let rest for 10 to 15 minutes. There's minimal fat to remove, so just strain through a muslin-lined mesh strainer positioned over a medium pot (see page 28 for guidance). Press and squeeze on the solids to expel extra broth. Discard the solids. There should be about 8 cups (2 l) broth.

If using the broth right away, season with fish sauce and with extra salt or sugar (or maple syrup), if needed; see broth seasoning tips on page 29. For make-ahead pho, partially cover the unseasoned broth, let cool, then refrigerate for up to 3 days or freeze for up to 3 months; reheat and season before using.

Prep and assemble the bowls While the broth cooks, or about 30 minutes before serving, ready ingredients for the bowls. Soak the dried noodles in hot water until pliable and opaque; drain, rinse, and drain well. If using fresh noodles, untangle or separate them and snip as needed. (Extra noodle prep tips are on page 32.) Divide them among 4 soup bowls.

Fill a saucepan two-thirds full with water and bring to a boil over high heat. Use a slotted spoon to add the eggs (use more eggs if you are short on chicken meat). Cook at a boil for 7 to 9 minutes, frequently stirring to help center the yolks; use the lesser amount of time for runny yolks. When done, cool the eggs in an ice bath for 5 to 10 minutes, then remove and let cool at room temperature. Reserve the pot of water.

Peel and halve the eggs. Line them up with the chicken, noodles, onion, green onion, cilantro, and pepper in a pho assembly line. Bring the broth to a simmer over medium heat as you assemble the bowls. If needed, add water to the former egg-boiling pot, then bring to a boil for the noodles.

For each bowl, place a portion of the noodles in a noodle strainer or mesh sieve and dunk the noodles in the boiling water. When the noodles are soft, 5 to 60 seconds, pull the strainer from the water, shaking it to drain excess water back into the pot. Empty the noodles into a bowl. Top with chicken and place the egg off to the side. Add onion, green onion, and cilantro. Finish with some pepper.

Recheck the broth flavor, then raise the heat to return it to a boil. Ladle about 2 cups (480 ml) broth into each bowl. Serve immediately with any extras.

Notes To make the broth in a 6- to 8-quart (6 to 8 l) pressure cooker, toast the spices in the cooker over medium heat. Add the ginger and onion. Stir until aromatic. Add 4 cups (1 l) water, and the chicken carcass, apple, vegetables, cilantro, and salt. Add another 4 (1 l) cups water. Bring to high pressure (15 psi) and cook for 15 minutes, or longer if the high setting is less than 15 psi. Naturally depressurize, rest for 15 minutes, then strain. The rest remains the same.

For **turkey pho**, use 2 pounds (900 g) roast turkey carcass, wings, drumsticks, and other uneaten parts. To prevent super cloudy broth, after breaking up the parts, quickly spray or rinse off impurities, especially in the backbone wells. Make the broth as usual. When done, retrieve and flush the turkey parts with water; drain, cool, and harvest the meat to top bowls. If you like, include halved boiled eggs or make turkey meatballs (page 96). Prep and assemble the bowls as usual. As a side dip for the meat, mix ½ cup (120 ml) cranberry sauce with 1 to 2 tablespoons Chile Sauce (page 103) or sriracha.

phở hải sản
SEAFOOD PHO

Serves 4

———

Takes about 45 minutes, plus 1¼ hours to simmer and cool

"I hope you don't make seafood pho for the book. It's not true pho," my mom said. Why not? I'd tried lobster and fish pho at Vietnamese restaurants in the United States and was surprised (and somewhat aghast) that they simply cooked the seafood in beef pho broth. The lesson learned from those experiences was this: seafood pairs well with pho spices.

To create a piscine pho noodle soup that isn't overly fishy, I opt for a vegetable broth seasoned with spices, dried and fresh shrimp, and bottled clam juice (the filtered liquid from steamed clams; the Bar Harbor brand is excellent). Ginger and seafood are great friends, so the aromatic root replaces black pepper for zingy heat. The finished pho is elegant, attractive, and delicious. Before making this recipe in a pressure cooker (see Notes), review the main recipe to get the gist of things.

BROTH

Chubby 2-inch (5 cm) section ginger, unpeeled

1 medium-large (9 oz | 270 g) yellow onion, unpeeled

3 ounces (90 g) Fuji apple, peeled, cored, and cut into thumbnail-size chunks

2 medium celery stalks (4 oz | 115 g total), coarsely chopped

1 large (6 oz | 180 g) carrot, cut into thick rounds (scrub and use unpeeled, if you like)

1 pound (450 g) napa cabbage leaves, halved lengthwise then cut crosswise into large pieces

2 star anise (16 robust points total)

1 inch (2.5 cm) cinnamon stick

1½ teaspoons fennel seeds

Heaping 1 teaspoon coriander seeds

9 cups (2.25 l) water

1 cup (240 ml) bottled clam juice

1½ teaspoons fine sea salt, plus more as needed

3 tablespoons dried shrimp

10 ounces (300 g) big shrimp, shells intact (select large, extra-large, or jumbo size)

1½ to 2 tablespoons fish sauce

About 1 teaspoon organic sugar, or 2 teaspoons maple syrup (optional)

BOWLS

10 ounces (300 g) dried narrow flat rice noodles, or 1 pound (450 g) fresh pho noodles (see page 19)

Cooked shrimp from the broth

10 ounces (300 g) fish fillet, such as rockfish, snapper, sea bass, tilapia, paiche, or salmon

½ small (2 oz | 60 g) yellow or red onion, thinly sliced against the grain and soaked in water for 10 minutes

2 thinly sliced green onions, green parts only

¼ cup (.2 oz | 5 g) chopped fresh cilantro, leafy tops only

1 teaspoon finely chopped peeled ginger

Optional extras: Garnish Plate for 4 (page 100), Chile Sauce (page 103), Saté Sauce (page 105), Garlic Vinegar (page 106)

Make the broth Char, peel, and prep the ginger and onion as instructed on page 30. Set aside with the apple, celery, carrot, and cabbage.

Put the star anise, cinnamon, fennel, and coriander in a small stockpot, about 8-quart (8 l) capacity. Over medium heat, toast the spices for several minutes, shaking or stirring, until fragrant. Add 4 cups (1 l) of the water to arrest the

continued

cooking process. Add the ginger and onion along with the apple and vegetables, salt, and dried shrimp. Pour in the remaining 5 cups (1.25 l) water and the clam juice.

Partially cover and bring to a boil over high heat. Meanwhile, peel and devein the shrimp. Toss the shrimp shells into the stockpot. Cover and refrigerate the shrimp for later use.

When the broth reaches a boil, uncover and lower the heat to gently simmer for 1 hour. (There's usually no scum to skim.) At the 50-minute mark, add the reserved shrimp to the pot; use a noodle strainer or mesh sieve and work in batches to retrieve them easily. Cook until just curled into a C shape, then transfer to a bowl to cool. If not serving soon, cover and refrigerate.

When the broth is done, let rest for 5 to 10 minutes, uncovered, before straining through a muslin-lined mesh strainer positioned over a medium pot (see page 28 for guidance). Press and squeeze on the solids to expel extra broth. Discard the solids. There should be about 8 cups (2 l).

If using the broth right away, season with fish sauce and, if desired, with extra salt and sugar (or maple syrup); see seasoning tips on page 29. When cooking in advance, partially cover the unseasoned broth, let cool, then refrigerate for up to 3 days or freeze for up to 3 months; season before using.

Prep and assemble the bowls While the broth cooks, or about 30 minutes before serving, ready ingredients for the bowls. Soak the dried noodles in hot water until pliable and opaque. Drain, rinse, and drain well. If using fresh noodles, untangle or separate them and snip as needed. (See page 32 for details.) Divide the noodles among 4 soup bowls.

If the shrimp are extra-large or jumbo size, cut each into manageable pieces: lay it flat on your work surface, steady it with one hand while cutting it from the back to the belly. You'll get 2 thin, nearly identical pieces. Otherwise, keep the shrimp whole.

If the fish fillet has skin attached, remove it first (see Notes for tips). Cut the fish flesh into broad, thin pieces; hold your knife at an angle as if you're cutting sushi. Set aside.

Set the onion, green onion, cilantro, and ginger alongside the noodles, shrimp, and fish to form a pho assembly line. Bring the broth to a simmer over medium heat. At the same time, fill a pot with water and bring to a rolling boil for the noodles.

For each bowl, place a portion of the noodles in the strainer or sieve and dunk in the boiling water. When the noodles are soft, 5 to 60 seconds, pull the strainer from the pot, shaking it to release excess water. Empty the noodles into a bowl. Arrange the shrimp and the fish on top. Add the onion, green onion, cilantro, and ginger.

Check the broth flavor, raise the heat, and bring it to a boil. Ladle about 2 cups (480 ml) broth into each bowl, then serve immediately with any extras.

Notes To make the broth with a pressure cooker, use a 6- to 8-quart (6 to 8 l) cooker. Peel the ginger, cut into thick slices, and smack; halve and cut the onion into thick slices. Over medium heat, toast the spices in the cooker. Add the ginger and onion; stir until aromatic. Add 4 cups (1 l) water. Then add the vegetables, apple, salt, dried shrimp, shrimp shells, 3 cups water (720 ml l), and clam juice. Lock the lid in place. Bring to high pressure (15 psi), adjust the heat, then cook for 15 minutes. Depressurize naturally. Remove the lid and reheat the cooker to poach the shrimp. Cool the broth for 5 minutes, then strain, season, and follow the rest of the recipe.

To remove the skin from a fish fillet, lay it skin side down on your work surface. Run your finger along one of the edges to separate the flesh from the skin and form a gap. Slide a boning or fillet knife in the gap, then saw and push the knife all the way through from one end (or side) to the other. Discard the skin.

phở thịt cừu
LAMB PHO

Serves 8

———

Takes about 1 hour, plus 3½ hours to simmer and cool

For a departure from beef pho soup, brew one with lamb. (Viet people traditionally enjoy goat, but in the States, it's not as accessible as its ruminant kin.) I blend beef leg bones and lamb neck bones to produce broth that's balanced and not overly gamey, which would be un-pho-like. The neck yields plenty of chopstick-tender meat for soup bowls and other dishes, such as the bonus lamb "pho-nitas" in Notes.

Lamb varies in flavor, and if yours is supergamey, add more spices; if it is delicate, initially lower the spices. Page 20 has tips on tweaking pho spices. Add lamb meatballs to the bowls for variety, or get fancy with rare lamb slices. Hoisin and chile sauces are great extras, as is fresh mint.

BROTH

Chubby 4-inch (10 cm) section ginger, unpeeled

1 pound (450 g) yellow onion, unpeeled

3 pounds (1.35 kg) beef marrow and knuckle bones (see page 37 for bone blending)

3 pounds (1.35 kg) meaty lamb necks

5½ quarts (5.5 l) water

1 to 1¼ pounds (450 to 565 g) boneless leg of lamb, cut into 2 pieces

6 star anise (48 robust points total)

3 medium (3 in | 7.5 cm) cinnamon sticks

9 whole cloves

1 very large Chinese black cardamom, whacked open with a meat mallet

Generous 1 tablespoon fennel seeds

Rounded 1½ tablespoons coriander seeds

1½ tablespoons fine sea salt

7⁄10 ounce (20 g) Chinese yellow rock sugar, or 1 large (8 oz | 225 g) Fuji apple, peeled, cored, and cut into thumbnail-size chunks

About ¼ cup (60 ml) fish sauce

About 2 teaspoons organic sugar, or 1 tablespoon maple syrup (optional)

BOWLS

1¼ pounds (565 g) dried narrow flat rice noodles, or 2 pounds (900 g) fresh pho noodles (see page 19)

Cooked lamb from the broth

8 ounces (225 g) boneless leg of lamb, 16 lamb meatballs (page 96, see Notes), or some of each (optional)

½ medium (3 oz | 90 g) yellow or red onion, thinly sliced against the grain and soaked in water for 10 minutes

3 or 4 thinly sliced green onions, green parts only

½ cup (.35 oz | 10 g) chopped fresh cilantro, leafy tops only

Pepper (optional)

Optional extras: Garnish Plate for 8, Homemade Hoisin, Chile Sauce, Saté Sauce, Garlic Vinegar (pages 100 to 106)

Make the broth Char, peel, and prep the ginger and onion as instructed on page 30. Set aside.

For clear broth, parboil and rinse the beef and lamb bones; see page 28 for guidance and use a 12-quart (12 l) stockpot. Rinse off impurities, quickly scrub the pot, then return the bones to the pot.

Pour in the water. Partially cover and bring to a boil over high heat. Uncover and lower the heat to gently simmer. Use a ladle or skimmer to remove any scum that rises to

continued

the top. Add the ginger, onion, and boneless lamb. Add the star anise, cinnamon, cloves, black cardamom, fennel and coriander seeds, salt, and rock sugar (or apple). Adjust the heat to gently simmer, uncovered, for 3 hours.

At the 1¼-hour mark, remove the boneless lamb; it should feel very firm. Transfer to a bowl and soak in water to cover for 10 minutes to prevent drying. Set aside to cool completely, then transfer the lamb to a bowl, cover, and refrigerate. Save the water bowl to reuse.

When the broth is done, use tongs to remove the lamb neck pieces and soak in the reserved water for 10 minutes. Drain, cool for 15 minutes, then pull the meat off the bones. Discard the bones and add the meat to the cooked leg pieces.

By now, the broth will have sufficiently rested to settle the impurities and concentrate the flavor. If you like, retrieve the beef bones from the pot and soak in water for 10 minutes; drain and harvest the tendon. Otherwise, discard the solids.

Skim some fat from the broth, then strain through a muslin-lined mesh strainer positioned over a large pot; see page 28 for guidance. Discard lingering solids. There should be 4 quarts (4 l).

If using the broth right away, season it with the fish sauce, extra rock sugar (if needed), and sugar (or maple syrup), if using; broth seasoning tips are on page 29. Or, partially cover the unseasoned broth, let cool, then refrigerate for up to 3 days or freeze up to for 3 months; reheat and season before using.

Prep and assemble the bowls About 30 minutes before serving, ready ingredients for the bowls. Soak dried noodles in hot water until pliable and opaque; drain, rinse, and drain well. If using fresh noodles, untangle or separate them and snip as needed. (More noodle prep tips are on page 32.) Divide the noodles among 8 soup bowls.

Thinly slice the cooked lamb leg; cut or pull the tender neck meat into bite-size pieces. If using, thinly slice the raw lamb (see page 94 for tips) and/or prep the meatballs as directed in their recipe. Cover if not using in 15 minutes.

Place the onion, green onion, and cilantro in separate bowls and line them up with the noodles, lamb, and pepper for a pho assembly line. Bring the broth to a simmer over medium heat. At the same time, fill a pot with water and bring to a rolling boil for the noodles.

For each bowl, place a portion of the noodles in a noodle strainer or mesh sieve and dunk in the boiling water. When the noodles are soft, 5 to 60 seconds, lift the strainer from the pot, shaking it to force excess water back into the pot. Empty into a bowl. Top with cooked lamb and any other meat toppings. Add onion, green onion, cilantro, and pepper.

Retaste the broth, then raise the heat and bring it to a boil. Ladle about 2 cups (480 ml) broth into each bowl. Serve immediately with any extras.

Notes If boneless leg of lamb is unavailable for broth, substitute ground lamb; break it into large chunks and cook in the broth for the entire 3 hours, then discard. The neck bones yield plenty of meat for the bowls.

To make lamb "pho-nitas," use the neck meat and a medium nonstick skillet. Add about 10 ounces (300 g) of the meat to cover the bottom and enough broth to cover by ½ inch (1.25 cm). Cook over medium heat for about 10 minutes, poking and mashing the meat as it softens. When the broth evaporates, add a good tablespoon of lamb pho fat (or neutral oil). Gently fry, stirring, to coax a dark brown finish and crisp bits. Season with pinches of salt, black pepper, and maybe Pho Spice Blend (page 111). Sprinkle in fish sauce for savory depth. Let rest for a few minutes to allow the flavors to meld before using for banh mi (see opposite), fried rice, tacos, or the like.

bánh mì thịt phở
BEEF PHO BANH MI

**Makes
6 sandwiches**

**Takes about
1 hour**

Several American chefs have created pho dip sandwiches, so why shouldn't you? I make mine based on a pot roast recipe from *James Beard's American Cookery*. The recipe worked for re-creating my favorite beef dip sandwich served at Philippe The Original in Los Angeles, and it also worked for this Vietnamese-American twist.

Using a pressure cooker instead of the oven to cook the beef saves time without changing the flavor much. The beef slices neatly for sandwiches once it has cooled, so cook it ahead of time. Kept uncut, the beef stores well in the fridge for days, perfect for a party (add beer on ice for a Viet-style beverage) or solo sandwich lunches.

If you have *The Banh Mi Handbook*, try the sriracha mayo and the daikon and carrot pickle, citrusy red cabbage pickle, or pickled shallot in the sandwich. Or, just use purchased mayo and pickled bean sprouts, as I have here. See Notes for an oven method.

BEEF

2¼ pounds (1 kg) boneless beef chuck or cross-rib roast, cut into 2 pieces

½ teaspoon fine sea salt

½ teaspoon pepper

1½ teaspoons light or dark brown sugar

1 medium (7 to 8 oz | 210 to 225 g) yellow onion, halved and cut into thick slices

Chubby 1½ inch (3.75 cm) section ginger, peeled, cut into chunks, and smashed

3 star anise (24 robust points total)

4 whole cloves

1 medium (3 in | 7.5 cm) cinnamon stick

1 tablespoon canola or other neutral oil

1⅔ cups (390 ml) water

2 tablespoons fish sauce

SANDWICHES

2½ cups (10 oz | 300 g) Pickled Bean Sprouts (page 143)

6 baguette-style rolls, bolillo rolls, or other light, suitable bread

Mayonnaise

Maggi Seasoning sauce (optional)

2 jalapeño or Fresno chiles, thinly sliced

1 small English cucumber, cut into rounds, ovals, or seeded strips

½ cup (about .5 oz | 15 g) coarsely chopped fresh cilantro, mint, and/or Thai basil leaves

Cook the beef Season the beef with the salt, pepper, and brown sugar. Set aside near the onion and ginger. Put the star anise, cloves, and cinnamon in a 6-quart (6 l) pressure cooker. Over medium heat, toast for several minutes, shaking or stirring, until fragrant. Add the onion and ginger. Stir for 45 to 60 seconds, until aromatic. Slide to a cool burner, then transfer to a large bowl.

Reheat the cooker over medium-high heat. Add the oil and swirl to coat. Add the beef and brown on all sides, 3 to 5 minutes total. Transfer and hold with the spices and aromatics. Add the water to the cooker to deglaze. Add the fish sauce, then replace the beef. There should be enough liquid to come about one-third of the way up the side of the meat. Add the spices, ginger, and onion, pushing them down around the beef.

Lock the lid in place. Bring to high pressure (15 psi) over high heat on a gas or induction stove, or medium heat on an electric stove. Lower the heat to maintain pressure, signaled by a gentle, steady flow of steam coming out of the cooker's valve. Cook for 30 minutes, or longer if your cooker's high setting is less than 15 psi.

continued

If serving soon, make the pickled bean sprouts while the beef cooks. Otherwise, make them up to 2 hours before you make the sandwiches.

When the beef is done, slide to a cool burner. Let the pressure decrease naturally, about 10 minutes. Remove the lid, tilting it away from you to avoid the hot steam. The beef should be chewy but reasonably tender; poke with a fork to test. If not, replace the lid and cook for another 5 minutes, releasing pressure through the steam vent or under cold running water. Remove the beef, loosely cover to prevent drying, and let cool until warmish to make slicing easier.

Strain the cooking liquid through a fine-mesh strainer into a shallow saucepan, discarding the solids; lining the strainer with muslin isn't necessary since a superclear broth isn't key. If needed, defat as you would a pho broth (see page 28 for details).

To achieve a concentrated pho flavor to later season the meat and bread, boil the liquid for 5 to 8 minutes, until reduced by one-third to one-half of its original volume. Taste to check the flavor. Take off heat and cover. (Or, cool and then refrigerate the liquid and beef separately for up to 3 days.)

Assemble the sandwiches Crisp the bread in a preheated 325°F (160°C) toaster oven or regular oven for 3 to 6 minutes; if the bread is very soft, rub the crust with wet hands to moisten before crisping at 350°F (180°C) for about 7 minutes. Meanwhile, thinly slice the beef across the grain and warm in the cooking liquid over medium-low heat to moisten and soak up flavor.

Briefly cool the bread, then slit lengthwise and hollow out some of the insides to make room for the filling. Line the bread with mayonnaise. Drizzle the cooking liquid or Maggi Seasoning sauce on the mayo for umami notes. Working from the bottom up, line each sandwich with the beef, a handful of pickled bean sprouts, 3 or 4 chile slices, 4 to 6 pieces cucumber, and 1 to 2 tablespoons herbs. Serve whole or cut in half crosswise. Offer extra pickled bean sprouts and the remaining cooking liquid on the side.

Notes To cook the beef in the oven, use a 5- to 6- quart (5 to 6 l) Dutch oven or lidded casserole to hold the meat comfortably. Position a rack in the middle of the oven and preheat to 325°F (160°C). Follow the instructions to ready the beef, spices, and aromatics. Brown the meat and deglaze the pan, add the fish sauce, and then replace the meat and other ingredients. Bring to a simmer on the stove, then cover and slide into the oven to cook for about 2 hours. Turn the beef at the 1-hour mark. Test for doneness with a fork. The rest of the recipe remains the same.

For a vegetarian banh mi, swap out the beef for Pan-Seared Tofu (page 97) or Pho Tempeh (page 99).

4

PHO ADD-ONS

Pho noodle soup can be a simple affair, but it may also be dolled up to the extreme. This chapter offers ideas for embellishing your bowls. Some of the recipes will seem straight forward and familiar, while others are based on my Vietnam travels and imagination. Make one, some, or all of the condiments and sauces. They keep well and have uses beyond pho.

thịt tái
THINLY SLICED STEAK

Serves 4 to 8, depending on recipe

Takes about 20 minutes

Ultratraditional pho has just broth, noodles, and cooked beef. It's lovely and pure. Adding sliced steak to make *phở tái chín* signals an upgrade. To prevent the raw beef from clouding up the broth, in Vietnam it is often lightly cooked in a ladle of hot broth before being added to the bowl. Stateside pho shops usually array raw paper-thin beef slices on the noodles and let the hot broth cook the beef. If you like medium-rare or rare beef, slice it superthin (think carpaccio) and present as a side for guests to dip into their bowls, where it will cook gently.

What cut to use? I prefer flavorful steak cuts like top sirloin, bottom sirloin (tri-tip), and New York strip; marbling is always welcomed. Avoid mild and lean eye of round. Filet mignon is very tender but lacking in beefy flavor.

The quantity below assumes that you'll have cooked beef in the bowl, too. Double the amount when steak is the only star. If there are meatballs (see opposite) along with cooked beef and steak, use a little less. Not much is needed: Thinly slicing is key to making a little meat go a long way.

For 4 servings: 4 to 5 ounces (115 to 150 g) well-trimmed beef steak

For 8 servings: 8 to 10 ounces (225 to 300 g) well-trimmed beef steak

For very thin slices, use a sharp thin-blade knife such as a Japanese santoku. As needed, cut the steak into chunks the size of a Roma tomato, about 2 by 3 inches (5 by 7.5 cm). Place on a plate and freeze for 15 minutes, or until firm on the outside. Identify the grain of the meat (which direction the muscle fibers are running), then cut across the grain to create slices a scant ⅛ inch (3 mm) thick. If the steak softens as you cut, return it to the freezer for a few minutes.

The sliced beef is best used at or near room temperature so it will be cooked by the boiling broth. Cover it to prevent drying if you don't use it within 15 minutes of cutting. It can be refrigerated for up to 24 hours; let it warm up to room temperature for bowl assembly.

Notes To render thick slices thin or to tenderize the beef, do as cooks in Vietnam do: whack each slice one or two times with the broad side of a heavy cleaver or chef's knife.

For extra aroma, add a little peeled and minced ginger to each bowl along with the onion and cilantro garnish. For thinly sliced Wagyu beef or rib eye, shop at a Japanese or Korean market.

bò viên
BEEF MEATBALLS

Makes about 24 meatballs

Takes about 30 minutes

Delicate and slightly snappy meatballs add visual, textural, and flavor pop to a bowl of pho. You can buy these meatballs at Asian markets, but they're easy to make, taste great, and freeze well.

Traditionally, lean meat was hand pounded into a paste, then seasoned and cooked. My modern shortcut is a full-size food processor. Achieving just the right texture—fine, smooth, and a bit springy, not rubber-band bouncy—involves plenty of starch, a gentle poaching, and an ice bath. For a strong beefy flavor, use what you'd select for a first-class burger. Omit the garlic if you don't like the bite, which mellows once the meatballs are warmed in broth. Use potato starch instead of cornstarch to yield a slightly more delicate texture.

For a combo pho bowl with cooked beef, use two meatballs per serving; when there's sliced cooked and raw beef, use one meatball per serving. You can also just serve two or three meatballs in a small bowl of pho broth with a garnish of green onion and cilantro or Vietnamese coriander (*rau răm*). See Notes for four variations.

1 clove garlic, minced and mashed with a knife or put through a press

½ teaspoon pepper

1 teaspoon baking powder

1½ teaspoons sugar

1 teaspoon toasted sesame oil

2 tablespoons potato starch or cornstarch

2 tablespoons fish sauce

3 tablespoons water

1 pound (450 g) ground chuck or 85 percent lean ground beef

Splash of canola oil or other neutral oil

Put the garlic, pepper, baking powder, sugar, sesame oil, starch, fish sauce, and water into the bowl of a food processor. Pulse several times to blend the seasonings. The lid often gets splattered, so remove the plunger to drop in chunks of ground beef through the feed tube. Run the machine until a rough ball forms around the blade. Let sit for 3 to 5 minutes to hydrate and season the meat.

Meanwhile, smear some canola oil on a platter or small baking sheet. Set aside for holding the meatballs.

When the meat is done resting, process the mixture for about 1 minute to achieve a relatively smooth, stiff paste. Pause to scrape the sides as needed. Transfer to a bowl.

Flatten the top with a spatula to compact, then divide into 4 wedges (each will yield about 6 meatballs).

To make a meatball, use two small spoons to scoop up about 1½ tablespoons of the meatball mixture. Pass it back and forth between the spoons to compact and shape into a meatball a generous 1 inch (2.5 cm) wide. Deposit on the oiled platter (or baking sheet). You'll have about 24 total when done. Slightly oil your hands, then roll each into a smooth, lightly shiny meatball. Loosely cover to prevent drying.

Fill a pot with water to a depth of your index finger, about 2½ inches (6.25 cm). Bring to a boil over high heat, then lower the heat to low. Have a bowl of ice water nearby.

Add the meatballs to the pot until they cover the bottom. (Do this in batches, if needed.) Raise the heat to medium and give the pot a stir or two to nudge the meatballs around.

They'll quickly or slowly float to the surface. Regardless, aim to gently poach them until they swell by about 25 percent and are just cooked through; if you cut one to check, a slight pink or purple in the center is okay. The cooking may take as long as 10 minutes.

continued

BEEF MEATBALLS, continued

When done, scoop the meatballs from the pot and drop into the ice water; let cool for about 3 minutes before transferring to a bowl or container to finish cooling. Meanwhile, repeat as needed to poach the remaining meatballs.

To use the meatballs, halve or quarter each one. As you're assembling the bowls, drop them in the broth to reheat for a few minutes before adding them to the bowls; a hard boil can toughen the meatball. Cooked meatballs can be refrigerated for up to 3 days or frozen for up to 3 months (thaw before using).

Notes It's customary to serve hoisin and chile sauces (see pages 102 and 103, respectively) with these meatballs. As you eat, give the meatball a dip in sauce to add bold accents of flavor.

For **beef and tendon meatballs**, reserve about 2 ounces (60 g) cooked tendon from the beef bones after brewing pho broth; you can refrigerate it, if you like, for up to 3 days before using. Cut the tendon into pieces the size of large peas or blueberries. Before blending the seasonings in the food processor, use it to finely chop the tendon; some pieces may refuse to get chopped, so finish the work by hand. Hold in a bowl. After the beef paste forms, add the tendon and let the machine work it in.

When making **lamb meatballs**, substitute ground lamb for the beef. To slightly offset lamb's gaminess, include 1 rounded teaspoon Pho Spice Blend (page 111) with the seasonings.

To make **chicken meatballs**, substitute ground dark-meat chicken (thigh meat) for the beef. Omit or use half as much garlic because chicken is delicate. Reduce the water to 2 tablespoons because ground chicken has more moisture than ground beef. Employ ground turkey thigh and the full amount of garlic to make terrific **turkey meatballs**; use 2½ tablespoons water in the mixture.

Regardless of the protein substitute, follow the cooking instructions in the main recipe.

đậu phụ chiên
PAN-SEARED TOFU

**Makes 8 pieces
(about 10 oz | 300 g)**

**Takes about
15 minutes**

Supereasy to make, this is a vegetarian convenience food (see photo, page 98) that I keep on hand for adding to noodle soup, stir-fries, fried rice, and rice paper rolls. It's tasty and healthier than deep-fried tofu, albeit not as rich. Sometimes I eat the pan-seared tofu as is, right out of the fridge. The initial cooking in a dry skillet efficiently rids the tofu of surface moisture so you don't have to blot or drain the tofu beforehand.

1 (14 oz | 420 g) block
extra-firm tofu

1 tablespoon regular
soy sauce

About 1 tablespoon canola
or other neutral oil

Cut the block of tofu crosswise into 2 pieces, then cut each piece crosswise into 4 thick pieces; imagine big dominoes or Zippo lighters. You'll have 8 pieces total. Put into a medium or large nonstick skillet. Drizzle in the soy sauce and coat both sides.

Cook over medium heat until sizzling, seared, and dry looking, about 5 minutes. There will be little moisture visible in the skillet. Drizzle the oil over the tofu, then use a spatula to flip the pieces.

Let cook for 4 to 5 minutes to sear and brown the second side. Shake the skillet to check if the tofu will dislodge from the bottom. When there is a little movement, use a spatula to flip the tofu over to add extra color and character to the first side, if needed. Aim for a rich, mottled brown surface with dark brown edges. When satisfied, transfer to a rack to cool and dry for about 5 minutes before using.

Notes The tofu can be refrigerated for up to 5 days. Let warm up to room temperature before using. Gently refry to return a bit of crispness to the tofu, if you like.

PHO TEMPEH

Makes 8 ounces
(225 g)
—
Takes about
20 minutes

Along with the Pan-Seared Tofu (page 97), this tempeh is among the meatless treats often in my fridge. Tempeh is not a traditional Viet ingredient, but I love to include it in vegetarian pho soup, where it soaks up the broth. I also crumble it for fried rice (pages 77 and 78), tuck it into banh mi sandwiches (page 89, Notes), and just snack on it.

Softening tempeh's texture and getting it to absorb other flavors is key to preparing it well. Some cooks steam it before using it in other dishes. I take a one-pan approach: Simmer sliced tempeh in pho broth to open up the fermented soybeans and lightly season them. The broth boils down and coats the exterior with concentrated flavor. The oil remaining in the pan gently fries the tempeh and gives it extra character.

Tempeh made with all soybeans best expresses the meaty, earthy quality of traditional tempeh and takes on the pho flavors well. Brands such as WestSoy and Lightlife are excellent and are sold at many supermarkets and natural foods stores.

8 ounces (225 g) tempeh

About 1 cup (240 ml) broth from Quick Vegetarian Pho (page 43), Vegetarian "Chicken" Pho (page 53), or Vegan "Beef" Pho (page 56)

Fine sea salt

Regular soy sauce, Maggi Seasoning sauce, or Bragg Liquid Aminos

Organic sugar or maple syrup

2 tablespoons canola or other neutral oil

Cut the tempeh crosswise into slices, each a scant ⅓ inch (8 mm) thick and as long as your thumb. If your tempeh is a rectangular slab, simply cut it crosswise. If the tempeh is a square slab, halve it crosswise, then cut the slices. Arrange as one layer, cut side down, in a medium nonstick skillet.

As needed, season the broth to create a good savory flavor, as if you were finishing it for bowl assembly. Stir in salt by the ⅛ teaspoon and soy sauce (or Maggi or Bragg) by the ½ teaspoon. If the broth becomes amber honey in color, add salt only to avoid darkening the tempeh too much with

soy sauce or other liquid seasonings. Add pinches of sugar or drops of maple syrup to refine flavors. When satisfied, pour the broth into the skillet and add the oil. There should be enough to cover the tempeh. Add extra broth (or water), if necessary.

Bring to a simmer over medium heat. Cook for 12 to 15 minutes, turning midway, until most of the broth disappears.

After things start gently sizzling, raise the heat slightly to fry the tempeh for 4 to 5 minutes, until richly browned here and there. The color depends on the broth used and your preference. The flavor mellows in pho broth and other dishes so the tempeh can finish looking bold. Wield chopsticks or a narrow spatula to turn the tempeh midway; be patient if it sticks. Add oil if things look dry.

Before using or storing, let the tempeh compose itself by cooling slightly or completely on a rack. It will keep refrigerated for up to 5 days.

đĩa rau sống

GARNISH PLATE

Serves 2

—

Takes 5 minutes

Depending on your pho philosophy, you can go supersimple or ornate with the tabletop pho garnishes. I keep things easy with regular spearmint (*húng*) from my garden and chiles that I've purchased or grown at home. Conventional limes can be bracing and take over pho flavors, so I prefer the Garlic Vinegar on page 106 for a light tang; ripe (yellow) Bearss lime and Meyer lemon are good, too. During the warmer months, I'll add Thai basil (*húng quế*) because it's at its peak; ditto for a type of spicy mint (*húng cay*) sold at Viet markets. When I'm in the mood for bean sprouts, I'll buy superfresh ones and blanch them to mellow their flavor and texture.

If you're hardcore, add *culantro* (*ngò gai*) leaves, a hot-weather herb with a strong, slightly sweet cilantro flavor; it's usually sold at Vietnamese, Latin, and Caribbean markets. In Saigon at the storied Pho Hoa on Pasteur Street, delicate sprigs of rice paddy herb (*ngò om*) are also included in the platter of garnishes set at each table. Sold at Vietnamese markets and traditionally used for southern Viet seafood soups, rice paddy herb adds a citrusy, cumin-like note to pho. Add or subtract as you like from this guideline. When needed, scale up for recipes in this book.

2 handfuls (about 3 oz | 90 g) bean sprouts

2 or 3 sprigs mint, regular or spicy

2 or 3 sprigs Thai basil

3 or 4 fresh culantro leaves

2 or 3 sprigs rice paddy herb

1 lime, cut into wedges

1 Thai chile or ½ jalapeño, Fresno, or serrano chile, thinly sliced

If you're blanching the bean sprouts, work it into the pho assembly process and use the pot set up for dunking noodles; the noodle strainer is perfect for the job. Blanch them before starting on the noodles to avoid giving them a starch bath, and put them on their own plate so they don't leak water on other garnishes. Otherwise, arrange the raw sprouts with the herbs and lime on a communal plate.

If the chile is small, cut it at a sharp angle to yield largish slices that can be easily identified in the bowl. Put the slices in a little dish so they don't get lost. Before bowl assembly, set the garnishes at the table with any other sides and condiments so you can dive in immediately.

HOT CHILE TIPS

Fresh hot chiles don't always deliver their spicy punch because of factors like weather. When it's cold outside, they have less oomph, so add extra to your pho bowls and dishes. Be careful during the summer months when their heat is on. Most of a chile's heat is contained in the capsaicin glands (membranes) attached to the seeds. Enjoy slices close to the stem if you're a heat seeker.

During prep, use the cut stem end to scoot chile pieces onto a knife blade and push them into wherever they're needed. Wash your hands with coarse salt if you touch a chile's cut surfaces.

SPICY MINT

CULANTRO

BEAN SPROUTS

RICE PADDY HERB

FRESNO CHILE

LIME

SERRANO CHILE

JALAPEÑO

SPEARMINT

THAI CHILE

THAI BASIL

tương ăn phở
HOMEMADE HOISIN

**Makes about
1 cup (240 ml)**

—

**Takes 10 minutes,
plus 15 minutes
to cool**

If you're going to tackle making pho, go the Full Monty and whip up your own pho hoisin sauce (see photo, page 104). It's easy and remarkable tasting, less sweet and more complex than the commercial product in the squirt bottle. Plus, you can dial in flavors to your liking.

I channel pho via my Pho Spice Blend and employ Japanese miso, a kin of Vietnamese fermented bean sauce. For a handsome and tasty outcome, select a dark miso, such as red, brown rice, or Hatcho; shop for miso at natural foods grocers and Asian markets. The soybean paste determines the color and flavor complexity. In general, the darker the better. A little rice flour, such as Bob's Red Mill or Mochiko Blue Star brand, acts as a binder.

Aside from enjoying this hoisin with pho noodle soup, I use it just like regular hoisin, in *char siu* pork or chicken marinades and sauces like the one for Rice Paper Salad Rolls (page 135).

1 large clove garlic, smacked with the broad side of a knife

⅛ teaspoon ground cayenne, or ¼ teaspoon dried red pepper flakes

½ teaspoon Pho Spice Blend (page 111)

2 teaspoons rice flour (sweet, regular, or brown rice)

1 tablespoon plus 1 teaspoon tahini

1 tablespoon plus 1 teaspoon unseasoned Japanese rice vinegar

⅓ cup (90 ml) water

⅓ cup (3 oz | 90 g) dark miso paste, such as brown rice, red, or Hatcho miso

½ cup (3.25 oz | 100 g) firmly packed light or dark brown sugar

Regular soy sauce, to taste

In a small, 1½-quart (1.5 l) saucepan, combine the garlic, cayenne (or pepper flakes), pho spice blend, rice flour, tahini, vinegar, water, miso, and sugar. Whisk or vigorously stir to combine well. Because miso varies so much in flavor, add up to 1 tablespoon of miso if the mixture is too mild or mellow.

Bring to a simmer over medium heat and cook, stirring occasionally, until thickened, about 1 minute. Let cool and concentrate off heat for 15 minutes; whisk or stir occasionally to prevent a skin from forming. Taste and, if needed, add soy sauce by the teaspoon or vinegar by the ½ teaspoon.

If the mixture is smooth, strain through a mesh strainer, discarding the garlic. If the mixture is chunky from the miso, puree it in a food processor. The flavors open up overnight, though you can enjoy the sauce right away. Keep refrigerated in a jar for up to 3 months, bringing to room temperature before using.

Notes Korean *doenjang*, or soybean paste, can be used instead of miso, but watch for the wheat if you are wheat intolerant. Chinese five-spice powder is a decent substitute for the spice blend. When you don't have time to make your own hoisin, purchase it (see page 26 for a buying guide).

tương ớt
CHILE SAUCE

**Makes about
¾ cup (180 ml)**

**Takes 20 minutes,
plus 1 hour
to cool**

In 2007, a waiter at a fancy, French-owned hotel in Saigon gifted me a great tip: Cholimex chile sauce. I'd had it with pho several mornings in a row and the moderately spicy-sweet sauce was perfect with the soup. Not as hot as Stateside sriracha, the Viet chile sauce went exceptionally well with Vietnamese food (as it should!). When the waiter showed me the bottle, he said, "I buy several six-packs for relatives whenever I go to America. It's sold all over town. Sister, go to Ben Thanh market."

I did and brought home a half-dozen bottles, mostly for me and my mom. They are long gone and Cholimex has yet to distribute in America. No problem. I came up with my own version (see photo, page 104). The tomato lends texture, balances the chile heat, and adds a slight, bright fruitiness. Choose fleshy, firm medium-hot chiles for a condiment with character.

1 large clove garlic

1 medium (3 to 4 oz |
   90 to 115 g) Roma tomato

6 ounces (180 g) Fresno chiles
   (about 8 medium)

Brimming ½ teaspoon
   fine sea salt

1 tablespoon sugar,
   preferably organic

1 tablespoon distilled
   white vinegar

½ cup (120 ml) water,
   plus more as needed

Coarsely chop the garlic and tomato. Transfer to a 1½-quart (1.5 l) saucepan, including the tomato juices and seeds.

Stem and quarter the chiles lengthwise. Because you want a moderate amount of heat, seed *half* of the chile pieces, reserving those unwanted parts in case the chiles are wimpy.

With the skin side facing up, coarsely cut all of the chiles crosswise into pieces the size of your thumbnail. Use one of the leftover stem pieces and your knife to usher them into the pan.

Add the salt, sugar, vinegar, and water. Bring to a brisk simmer over medium heat. Cook for 8 to 10 minutes, until the chiles have softened. Taste midway. If it's too mild, add some of the reserved chile seeds and spongy placenta to the pan. When done, slide to a cool burner, let sit for 3 to 5 minutes, then puree in a blender. Expect skin bits and seeds to remain.

Pass through a fine-mesh strainer, pressing on the mixture with a spatula; discard the solids. Allow to cool and concentrate, uncovered, for about 1 hour before tasting and tweaking. If needed, add salt by the pinch, sugar by the ¼ teaspoon, vinegar by the ½ teaspoon, or water by the tablespoon.

Texturally, the sauce should resemble a pourable sriracha. The flavor should be pleasantly sweet and spicy. You will want to eat the chile sauce by the spoonful but know that you should not. Keep refrigerated for up to 3 months. Enjoy at room temperature.

Notes Organic cane sugar perfectly balances and brightens the chile heat without being cloying. As an experiment, substitute ½ ounce (15 g) yellow Chinese rock sugar, which you may already have for preparing broth. If the chile sauce has too many rough edges, round them out with a touch of maple syrup.

When Fresno chiles aren't available, or if they're just not very hot, try red or green jalapeño. Consider combining different kinds of chiles, too.

HOMEMADE
HOISIN

GARLIC
VINEGAR

SATÉ
SAUCE

CHILE
SAUCE

sốt sa-tế
SATÉ SAUCE

**Makes about
1 cup (240 ml)**

—

**Takes about
20 minutes, plus
1 hour to cool**

Brownish red from chiles and sweet-savory from shallot, lemongrass, and dried shrimp, this addictively good condiment may be offered at pho restaurants as a special side or featured in a spicy lemongrass pho. Viet people call it *sốt sa-tế* (saté sauce), though it bears little resemblance to the Southeast Asian peanut sauce served with grilled meat skewers.

As a colony of China for close to a thousand years, Vietnam has taken many cultural cues from its northern neighbor, including this sauce, which is based on Chinese *sha-cha* sauce—ironically, a Chinese take on Southeast Asian saté sauce. This sauce isn't as ubiquitous as hoisin and chile sauce at Viet restaurants, but people who've tasted it tend to adore it. Make a batch to enjoy with pho soup or enliven vegetarian fried rice (page 78) or chicken and celery stir-fried noodles (page 115). You'll find many uses beyond this book. See Notes for a vegetarian version. To dial in the flavor, use weight measurements where provided. A full-size processor makes this a cinch, though a mini-prep processor will work, too.

½ ounce (15 g) dried shrimp

½ cup (1.4 oz | 40 g) coarsely chopped lemongrass (2 trimmed stalks)

1 tablespoon coarsely chopped garlic

Brimming ¼ cup (1.2 oz | 35 g) coarsely chopped shallot

2 tablespoons dried red pepper flakes

¾ cup (180 ml) canola or other neutral oil

1 tablespoon sugar, preferably organic

2 teaspoons regular soy sauce

1½ tablespoons fish sauce

To slightly soften the shrimp, rinse them under warm tap water. Drain, then chop into pea-size pieces. Whirl in a food processor to a fine, somewhat fluffy texture. Expect a few lingering pebbly bits.

Add the lemongrass to the processor and chop to tiny bits. Add the garlic and shallot and process to a minced consistency, pausing to scrape the sides as needed. Transfer to a 1½-quart (1.5 l) saucepan. Add the pepper flakes and oil and stir to combine. Bring to a simmer over medium-low heat. Let bubble and sizzle for 8 to 10 minutes, swirling or stirring occasionally. The mixture will seem thin and a bit loose.

Add the sugar, soy sauce, and fish sauce. Continue cooking for 5 minutes, stirring occasionally, until the mixture seems thick and buoyant under the weight of your spoon or spatula. Expect the bubbles to become bigger toward the end. Slide to a cool burner and cool completely before using or storing in a jar. The mixture will darken and concentrate in flavor as it rests. It will keep refrigerated for up to 3 months. Bring to room temperature and stir it well before using.

Notes For a **vegetarian saté sauce**, omit the shrimp. Use ¾ teaspoon fine sea salt instead of the fish sauce. Decrease the amount of oil to ⅔ cup (150 ml). Keep the same quantities for the lemongrass, shallot, garlic, red pepper flakes, sugar, and soy sauce. Cook for the same amount of time. You'll yield about ¾ cup (180 ml).

Dried shrimp is sold at Asian markets; see Notes on page 67 for a buying guide. In a pinch, substitute ³⁄₁₀ ounce (10 g) ground Mexican shrimp (*camaron molido*), usually sold in plastic packages at supermarkets near other Latin seasonings. The result is less refined, but it may save you a trip to an Asian market.

To trim lemongrass, chop off the tough bottom base with its hard core and the green, woody top section. Peel away loose or dry outer layers to reveal a smooth, tight stalk. The trimmed, usable section will be 4 to 8 inches (10 to 20 cm) long, depending on the original stalk's size. Prep as directed in the recipe.

dấm tỏi
GARLIC VINEGAR

**Makes about
¾ cup (180 ml)**

**Takes 5 minutes,
plus overnight
aging**

When I noticed this condiment at Hanoi pho restaurants in 2010, I was skeptical. Northern pho diehards usually don't add lime or the like to their bowls, so where did the garlic-infused vinegar come into play?

I asked a local who was around my age, and she said she'd always had it with pho. I sprinkled some into my beef pho and it added a wonderful, delicate bright note. The garlic didn't hit me on the head. It lent a pungent edge to the mild vinegary tang, which amplified the broth without taking it in a totally different direction as a squirt of lime would. The garlic vinegar was very northern Vietnamese in its subtle grace, and my skepticism turned to love.

For recipes in this book, this vinegar (see photo, page 104) works its magic on noodle soup, panfried and stir-fried noodles, fried rice, and dumpling dipping sauce. Overall, it's good for times when a dish needs a slightly tart top note to balance flavors; I've splashed it into greens toward the end of the cooking time. Hanoi cooks often slice or chop the garlic, but bruising the cloves prevents the garlic from wandering into your food.

2 cloves garlic, smacked with
the broad side of a knife

2 Thai chiles or 1 large
serrano chile, partially split
lengthwise

¼ cup (60 ml) unseasoned
Japanese rice vinegar

½ cup (120 ml) water

Combine all of the ingredients in a jar. Cover and age it in the refrigerator overnight.

The next day, check the flavor: The main zing ideally comes from the garlic, with the chile playing a minor supporting role. If the garlic or chile is too harsh, add more vinegar and water, starting with a 1:2 ratio. Increase or decrease the amount of garlic, depending on its pungency and your preference. For extra chile bite, double the quantity and see what happens.

You can use the vinegar the day after it's made. It keeps in the refrigerator for months, so feel free to tinker with it over time. For practicality and authenticity, present the condiment with a teaspoon for guests to help themselves.

Notes When the vinegar runs out, add new ingredients to the old ones in the jar. When things taste tired or off, start over.

nước mắm gừng
GINGER DIPPING SAUCE

**Makes ⅔ cup
(150 ml)**

—

**Takes 5 minutes,
plus 15 minutes
to rest**

Many people enjoy chicken pho with a side of this zippy sauce. They dip the flesh into the sauce as they eat the soup. The fresh ginger bite adds a last-minute layer of flavor that some find to be scintillating while others find to be distracting. Try it out and judge for yourself.

Beyond pho soup, this dipping sauce is fabulous with Chicken and Pho Fat Rice (page 81) and Spicy Chicken Slaw (page 142). Its tangy heat cuts richness and enlivens whatever it touches.

Rounded 2 tablespoons
    peeled and finely chopped
    ginger

6 tablespoons (90 ml)
    fresh lime juice

2 to 2½ tablespoons sugar

2 to 3 tablespoons fish sauce

2 teaspoons finely chopped
    seeded Fresno or
    jalapeño chile

In a small bowl, stir together the ginger, lime juice, and sugar to dissolve the sugar. Taste to make sure it's agreeable on a spicy-tart-sweet level. Adjust as needed. Add the fish sauce and chile and set aside for 15 minutes to meld and develop flavors. The sauce may be refrigerated for a few days. Serve in the bowl or use as a salad dressing.

bánh quẩy
FRIED BREADSTICKS

Makes 12
—
Takes 1 hour,
plus 4 hours or
up to overnight
to rest

My first trip back to Vietnam was in December 2002. In Hanoi, I found a cramped pho joint where locals sat on low wood benches slurping away at steamy bowls; everyone held their personal belongings on their laps. Two gentlemen across from us nodded approvingly as my non-Viet husband enjoyed his pho. They ate theirs with intermittent dips of Chinese fried breadsticks (called *yóutiáo* in Mandarin).

I was flummoxed. Why add the Asian equivalent of a churro, doughnut, and crouton to delicate pho? As it turned out, the practice began during the Vietnam War when food shortages led Hanoians to get creative with their meager pho. I tried it and found the breadsticks to be a deliciously fun pho friend.

You can buy frozen ones at Asian markets, but they come together easily with grocery store ingredients. Food-grade alum, sold at regular supermarkets for pickling, makes the breadsticks crisp. Some cooks employ baking ammonia (see Notes) for an extra leavening boost, but the odor takes too long to dissipate after frying. Weigh ingredients using metric units for consistent results. Gold Medal and Whole Foods flour worked well for this recipe, as did Calumet baking powder. This unusual dough comes together quickly, so be prepared.

¾ teaspoon (.15 oz | 4 g) baking soda

1 teaspoon (.2 oz | 5 g) food-grade alum

Scant 1 teaspoon (.2 oz | 5 g) fine sea salt

1½ teaspoons (.2 oz | 6 g) sugar

2 tablespoons (.9 oz | 26 g) baking powder

Brimming 1 cup (8 oz | 228 g) water

3½ teaspoons canola or other neutral oil, plus more for deep-frying

2½ cups (12.5 oz | 370 g) unbleached all-purpose flour

Make the dough Combine the baking soda, alum, salt, sugar, and baking powder in a mixing bowl. Add the water and 2 teaspoons of the oil (expect instant fizzing) and stir to dissolve. Add the flour and stir to combine into a ball that cleans the sides of the bowl. Let sit for 3 to 5 minutes to hydrate.

Smear 1 teaspoon oil on your work surface (wood is perfect) to prevent initial sticking. Transfer the dough ball to your work surface and knead until smooth and soft, 1 to 2 minutes. When the dough starts sticking, add a big pinch of flour to your work surface. The ideal dough is soft like pizza dough, a bit sticky, and feels slack. Press on the dough, and it should bounce back but leave an indent.

Divide in half and shape into 2 loaves. Very lightly coat each in the ½ teaspoon of oil and wrap separately in plastic wrap. Keep the slightly oiled work surface handy if you plan to reuse it later in the day for shaping breadsticks. Let the dough rest at room temperature for 4 hours or refrigerate overnight and bring to room temperature before using. Wrapping the dough helps it to relax, soften, and develop the right texture during frying. You can fry after resting for 2 or 3 hours, but the breadsticks won't expand as much.

Fry the breadsticks Situate your work surface near the stove. Very lightly flour your work surface. The dough may feel oddly cold, somewhat tacky and soft, even borderline beyond control. That's normal.

continued

Stretch and pat each piece of dough into a slab about 12 inches (30 cm) long, 3 inches (7.5 cm) wide, and ½ inch (1.25 cm) thick. Slide the dough on your work surface to make sure it is not sticking. Loosely cover and let rest for 10 minutes. Have a glass of water and a chopstick nearby.

Meanwhile, get the frying setup ready. Pour oil into a large wok or deep skillet to a depth of 1½ to 2 inches (3.75 to 5 cm). Heat over medium-high heat to slightly above 350°F (180°C); the ideal temperature is roughly 360°F (185°C). Place a cooling rack topped with a double layer of paper towels and a metal slotted spoon near the frying area.

Work with 1 dough slab at a time to shape the breadsticks. Use a knife to cut 12 crosswise strips, each about 1 inch (2.5 cm) wide and 3 inches (7.5 cm) long. If the strips are sticking to one another on the cut edges, quickly move every other one so they're no longer too close to one another.

Dip one end of the chopstick into the glass of water and use it to paint a light water line down the middle of *every other* dough strip. Put a dry dough strip atop a wet one. Use the dry end of the chopstick to *gently* press each pair of dough strips down the center line to make sure they stick together. Repeat with the other slab to form 12 pairs of strips total. Loosely cover to prevent drying.

When the oil approaches temperature, lower the heat slightly to steady it. Using both sets of thumbs and index fingers, pick up and stretch a pair of strips to about double its length, 6 to 8 inches (15 to 20 cm). Gently drop it into the oil. Repeat with the other pairs of dough strips, frying 3 or 4 per batch.

Once a breadstick floats to the top, use a slotted spoon to bathe its midline with oil and coax puffy expansion. Fry for 2 to 3 minutes, turning often, until golden brown. Drain on the towel-lined rack. Return the oil to temperature before frying the remaining strips. Cool slightly before eating.

Notes Fried breadsticks keep well for hours after frying. They can be refrigerated for 1 week or frozen for 2 months. When planning to store and reheat later, slightly underfry to a golden color, as they'll darken during reheating. Return them to room temperature, then refresh in a preheated 375°F (190°C) toaster oven for 3 to 5 minutes, turning when you hear gentle sizzling; to promote heat circulation and soak up excess oil, put the breadsticks on a paper towel set on the oven's rack (or use a rack set on a baking sheet).

For a tiny extra rise, replace the baking soda with ½ teaspoon (.1 oz | 3 g) baking soda and ½ teaspoon (.07 oz | 2 g) baking ammonia. If there is a strong ammonia smell after frying, let sit to dissipate (about 1 hour) before eating.

gia vị phở
PHO SPICE BLEND

Makes about
1½ tablespoons
—
Takes about
10 minutes

When you want to define as well as reinforce the pho imprint, use this spice blend. I formulated it for Homemade Hoisin (page 102), lamb meatballs (page 96), Pho Fried Rice (page 77), pot stickers (pages 129 and 131), and a Pho Michelada (page 153), but the applications are limitless. In fact, it's nice as a rub for roasted and grilled meats (see Notes). Try it instead of Chinese five-spice powder. Make a double batch if it grows on you.

Star anise may be whole or broken and varies in size. Gather fragrant, big points (the petal-shaped seed pods) for the best outcome. See page 20 for details on Chinese black cardamom.

2 star anise (16 robust points total), or 1 star anise (8 robust points total) and 1 medium Chinese black cardamom

2 whole cloves

½ teaspoon fennel seeds

1 teaspoon coriander seeds

10 black peppercorns

¼ teaspoon ground cinnamon

Break up the star anise as needed, dropping the points into a small saucepan, skillet, or wok. If using the black cardamom, use a meat mallet to crush and break the skin, then remove the seeds and add to the star anise; discard the skin since it won't grind up easily.

Add the cloves, fennel seeds, coriander seeds, and peppercorns. Toast over medium heat, stirring, for about 3 minutes, until fragrant and slightly darkened. Cool off heat and then grind to a fine texture in a clean spice grinder (a dedicated electric coffee grinder works great); if you like, hold on tight and shake the grinder to get all of the ingredients into contact with the blades. Add the cinnamon and pulse a few times to combine.

Transfer to a jar and keep in the cupboard for up to 1 month. Grind a tablespoon of raw rice to clean out the grinder.

Notes To make a rub for grilled or roasted pork or chicken, combine the spice blend with kosher salt in a 1:1 or 2:3 ratio. Mild-tasting coarse kosher salt disperses savoriness more evenly throughout the spices than fine sea salt or table salt.

5

STIR-FRIED, PANFRIED, AND DEEP-FRIED PHO

Pho means more than just flat rice noodles in fragrant broth. Wide noodles—
the width of pappardelle—are unwieldy in soup and are best cooked up in a wok
or skillet. Try stir-frying the noodles like Chinese *chow fun* or opt for something
more majestic: a panfried chewy-crisp pancake crowned with a saucy stir-fry.
If you're willing to get a little messy, batter coat and deep-fry the noodles into
fritters and top with a stir-fry.

    To execute these dishes well requires prepping and lining up the components
so they're ready to cook. If you do certain steps ahead, like cook the noodles,
things flow quickly and smoothly.

phở xào gà
SATÉ CHICKEN, CELERY, AND PHO NOODLES

Serves 4 to 6 as a side dish

—

Takes about 45 minutes

These noodles deliver a wallop of flavor via the spicy saté sauce (make it in advance!) and the celery itself. Traditional cooks would use slender Chinese celery sold at Asian markets, but regular celery delivers plenty of punch and crunch. Use vivid green celery and a handful of its leaves and tiny petiole stalks. I often look for relatively thin but superflavorful celery at farmers' markets.

In this and the next recipe, the noodles are slightly undercooked because they'll absorb more liquid and soften further during stir-frying. See Notes for a meatless version.

7 ounces (210 g) dried wide flat rice noodles, or 1 pound (450 g) fresh chow fun rice noodles (see page 19)

¼ teaspoon fine sea salt, plus more as needed

About 3 tablespoons canola or other neutral oil

8 ounces (225 g) boneless, skinless chicken thigh, cut across the grain into bite-size pieces

1 teaspoon cornstarch

Brimming ½ teaspoon toasted sesame oil

½ teaspoon dark soy sauce, or ½ teaspoon dark molasses and a big pinch of fine sea salt

2½ teaspoons fish sauce

3 teaspoons regular soy sauce

½ teaspoon sugar

1½ teaspoons Saté Sauce (page 105), plus more for serving

2 tablespoons water

1½ teaspoons peeled and minced ginger

3 large cloves garlic, finely chopped

½ small (2 oz | 60 g) red onion, cut along the grain into thick wedges

8 ounces (225 g) celery stalks, cut on a sharp diagonal into long, thin pieces

Small handful of celery leaves and their tiny petiole stalks (take from inner ribs, if necessary)

Garlic Vinegar (page 106, optional)

If using dried noodles, boil them in water for about 6 minutes, until cooked and just slightly firm. Drain, flush with cold water, and drain well. Transfer to a plate. Toss with the salt and 2 teaspoons of the canola oil. Spread out to dry and cool completely, about 15 minutes; cover if not using soon or refrigerate up to 3 days. If using fresh noodles, separate them into strands or layers and set aside.

In a bowl, combine the chicken, cornstarch, sesame oil, dark soy sauce (or molasses and salt), 1 teaspoon of the fish sauce, and 1½ teaspoons of the regular soy sauce. For the seasoning sauce, stir together the remaining 1½ teaspoons fish sauce and 1½ teaspoons regular soy sauce with the sugar, saté sauce, and water. Set the chicken and sauce by the stove.

To stir-fry, heat a large wok or nonstick skillet over medium-high. Swirl in 2 teaspoons of the canola oil. Add the ginger and garlic. Stir for 15 seconds, until aromatic, then push to the side. Increase the heat to high. Add the chicken, spreading it out into a single layer. Let cook, undisturbed, for about 1 minute, until the edges turn opaque. Flip and stir for about 1 minute, until barely cooked through. Transfer to a plate.

continued

Add the onion, celery, and celery leaves to the pan. Stir-fry for 1 to 2 minutes, until just softened; lower the heat and/or add a splash of water to facilitate cooking. Hold with the chicken.

Rinse and dry the pan. Reheat over high. Swirl in the remaining 1½ tablespoons canola oil. Add the noodles, spreading them out into a thick layer. Sear, undisturbed, for 1 minute, until a tad crusty. Bank to the side.

Return the chicken and vegetables to the pan. Stir to combine with the noodles, then pour in the seasoning sauce. Stir-fry for 1 minute to heat through and finish cooking the chicken. Transfer to a platter and serve. Invite guests to add punch via dabs of saté sauce and/or brightness via sprinklings of garlic vinegar.

Notes For a vegetarian **saté tofu, celery, and pho noodles**, thinly slice 5 or 6 pieces Pan-Seared Tofu (page 97) and season with a little salt. For the seasoning sauce, use ¼ teaspoon salt, ¼ teaspoon sugar, 2 to 3 teaspoons vegetarian Saté Sauce (page 105), 1½ tablespoons regular soy sauce, and 2 tablespoons water. Using 2 teaspoons canola oil in the pan, stir-fry the ginger, garlic, onion, celery and celery leaves over medium-high heat until slightly softened. Add the tofu, heat through, then hold on a plate. Wash and reheat the pan, add the remaining oil, cook the noodles, return the tofu and vegetables, then finish with the seasoning sauce. Serve with the extra condiments.

DECODING PHO SHOP NAMES

Vietnamese people love to display pride, nostalgia, and entrepreneurship in pho restaurant names, particularly those abroad. Many have numbers attached to them. Pho 54 generally refers to the historic partitioning of the country into North and South Vietnam in 1954. Pho 75 and Pho 79 likely signal people's personal histories, such as when they arrived in America or opened their business. For practical purposes, Pho 50 is located off U.S. Route 50 in Falls Church, Virginia. Pho #1 competitively shouts that it's better than the rest.

Restaurants such as Pho Pasteur, Pho Hoa, and Pho Hien Vuong remind diners of popular spots in Vietnam. Pho Tau Bay in New Orleans continues a pho family legacy that began in Saigon in the 1960s. Pho Bac proclaims northern (*bắc*) Vietnamese roots.

The owners of Pho 777 and Pho 888 are hoping for prosperity. Detroit's Pho Lucky was named after the owner's late son, Luc Ky. Viet people adore puns, which explains restaurants like Good Pho You, 9021Pho, and Pho Ever. Regardless of name, it's part of the pho-nomenon.

phở xào bò
BEEF, RAPINI, AND PHO NOODLES

Serves 4 to 6
as a side dish

—

Takes about
45 minutes

In Vietnam, people typically stir-fry pho noodles with beef and a mild mustard green that's the same as Cantonese *yu choy*. Those greens are an Asian market purchase, so I frequently substitute rapini (broccoli rabe). It has a nutty, slightly bitter flavor and gorgeous green color; to ensure quick cooking, I select tender rapini with stems no bigger than a fat pencil, about ⅓ inch (8 mm). Feel free to use another favorite fast-cooking green; blanched broccolini would work, too. The leek contributes a sweet lilt. Pho spice and tomato lend depth and dimension.

7 ounces (210 g) dried wide flat rice noodles, or 1 pound (450 g) fresh chow fun rice noodles (see page 19)

¼ teaspoon fine sea salt, plus more as needed

About 3 tablespoons canola or other neutral oil

8 ounces (225 g) well-trimmed beef top sirloin or flank steak, cut across the grain into slices 3 inches (7.5 cm) long and ¼ inch (6 mm) thick

1½ teaspoons peeled and minced ginger

1 teaspoon cornstarch

Brimming ½ teaspoon toasted sesame oil

2½ teaspoons fish sauce

3½ teaspoons regular soy sauce

½ teaspoon dark soy sauce, or ½ teaspoon dark molasses plus a big pinch of fine sea salt

½ teaspoon Pho Spice Blend (page 111)

½ teaspoon sugar

1 tablespoon water

¼ cup (60 ml) coarsely grated ripe Roma or regular tomato (use largest hole on a box grater)

4 cloves garlic, finely chopped

8 ounces (225 g) tender rapini, cut into pieces as long as an index finger

4 ounces (115 g) leek, white part only, cut into strips the length and width of an index finger

Garlic Vinegar (page 106, optional)

If using dried noodles, boil them in water for about 6 minutes, until cooked and just slightly firm. Drain, flush with cold water, and drain well. Transfer to a plate. Toss with the salt and 2 teaspoons of the canola oil. Spread out to dry and cool completely, about 15 minutes; cover if not using soon or refrigerate for up to 3 days. If using fresh noodles, separate them into strands or layers and set aside.

In a bowl, combine the beef, ginger, cornstarch, sesame oil, 1 teaspoon of the fish sauce, 1½ teaspoons of the regular soy sauce, and the dark soy sauce (or molasses and salt). For the seasoning sauce, stir together the remaining 1½ teaspoons fish sauce and 2 teaspoons regular soy sauce with the spice blend, sugar, water, and tomato. Set the beef and sauce by the stove.

To stir-fry, heat a large wok or nonstick skillet over medium-high. Swirl in 2 teaspoons of the canola oil. Add the garlic, stir for 15 seconds, until aromatic, then push aside to make room for the beef. Increase the heat to high. Add the beef, spreading it out into a single layer. Let cook, undisturbed, for about 1 minute. After the edges brown, flip and stir for 30 seconds, until barely cooked through. Transfer to a plate.

Add the rapini and leek and keep stir-frying for 1 to 2 minutes, until just softened; lower the heat and/or add a splash of water to facilitate cooking. When done, add to the beef.

Rinse and dry the pan. Reheat over high, then swirl in the remaining 1½ tablespoons canola oil. Add the noodles, spreading them out into a thick layer. Sear, undisturbed, for 1 minute, until a tad crusty. Bank to the side.

Return the beef and vegetables to the pan. Stir to combine with the noodles, then pour in the seasoning sauce. Stir-fry for 1 minute to heat through and finish cooking the beef. Pile onto a platter. Serve with the garlic vinegar and let guests sprinkle it on for a tangy lift.

phở xào dòn
PANFRIED PHO NOODLES

Serves 4 to 6 as a side dish

—

Takes about 1 hour, including the stir-fry

Chewy, crisp panfried pho noodle dishes date back to the 1930s in Hanoi. They're a Viet favorite at restaurants and at home. Fresh rice noodles yield fabulous results, but I've found that dried ones work well, too. Boil and oil dried noodles up to 3 days in advance and you can treat them like fresh ones. Since rice doesn't brown and crisp easily, the sugar and cornstarch coax crisping and coloring.

This master recipe outlines how to organize yourself to panfry the noodles, segue into stir-frying the topping, and then finish by assembling the dish. If you like, stir-fry the topping as the noodles panfry. There are three topping options from which to choose.

5 ounces (150 g) dried wide flat rice noodles, or 14 ounces (420 g) fresh chow fun rice noodles (see page 19)

3½ tablespoons canola or other neutral oil

Stir-fry topping: 1 full recipe Chicken, Mushroom, and Bok Choy (page 121), Beef, Shrimp, and Vegetables (page 123), or Tofu and Thai Basil (page 124)

Scant ½ teaspoon fine sea salt

½ teaspoon sugar

1 tablespoon cornstarch

About 1 tablespoon water

If using dried rice noodles, boil them in water for about 7 minutes, until just cooked. Drain, flush with cold water, and drain again. Transfer to a large plate or small baking sheet. Toss with 1½ teaspoons of the oil and then spread the noodles out to dry and cool completely, about 15 minutes. The noodles may be refrigerated for up to 3 days; bring to room temperature before seasoning and panfrying.

When starting with fresh rice noodles, do your best to separate the noodles into strands or layers (they may be sticky or hard). Set aside.

Prep the topping ingredients. Keep them by the stove so you can easily stir-fry them after panfrying the noodles.

Season the noodles just before panfrying. In a medium bowl, stir together the salt, sugar, cornstarch, and water; add the noodles and toss to coat. To panfry the noodles, use a 10-inch (25 cm) nonstick skillet and heat over medium or medium-high. Add about 2 tablespoons of the oil to film the bottom of the skillet. Add the noodles, spreading them into a large pancake. Let gently sizzle for 4 to 5 minutes, until light golden on the underside (check the rim or lift to peek) and stuck together as a nest of sorts.

Drizzle about 1 tablespoon of the oil on the noodles, then flip with a wide spatula or confident sharp jerk of the skillet handle. Fry the second side, adjusting the heat as needed, for 3 to 4 minutes, until crisp chewy and pale gold; some brown spots are okay. When done, slide the skillet into the oven to keep warm (there's no need to turn it on).

Stir-fry the topping as instructed in its recipe. When done, take off heat. Slide the noodles onto a serving plate, with the crispier and more handsome side up. Cut with kitchen scissors into 4 or 6 wedges. Top with the stir-fry and serve.

Notes If the noodles soften while waiting for the stir-fry, refry them over medium-high heat for 1 to 2 minutes to recrisp. If they dry out, refry with a splash of water and cover to rehydrate; add oil as needed to coax back crunchy chewiness.

phở rán dòn
DEEP-FRIED PHO NOODLES

Serves 4 to 6
as a side dish

—

Takes about
1 hour, including
the stir-fry

If you were to find pho at American county fairs, I imagine that the noodles would be coated in batter, fried into crunchy, fritter-like rafts, and then topped with a stir-fry. That's what I ate in Hanoi at a sidewalk joint that served nontraditional pho, including the pho noodle rolls on page 133. In Saigon, I'd had deep-fried pho noodles lightly coated in cornstarch, but they weren't as fun as the batter-coated kind.

This dish requires a smallish amount of noodles since there's batter to add heft. The noodles may be topped with any stir-fry as long as it's not too saucy, or the noodles will quickly lose their crunch. If you like, make extra cornstarch slurry for the stir-fry to cover last-minute tweaks.

4 ounces (115 g) dried wide flat rice noodles, or scant 12 ounces (350 g) fresh chow fun rice noodles (see page 119)

1 teaspoon canola or other neutral oil, plus more for deep-frying

Stir-fry topping: 1 full recipe Chicken, Mushroom, and Bok Choy (page 121), Beef, Shrimp, and Vegetables (page 123), or Tofu and Thai Basil (page 124)

¼ cup (1.25 oz | 35 g) all-purpose flour, bleached or unbleached

⅓ cup (1.5 oz | 45 g) cornstarch

1 teaspoon baking powder

½ teaspoon baking soda

¼ teaspoon fine sea salt

2 teaspoons sugar

6 tablespoons (90 ml) cold water (measure from a cup of ice water)

If using dried rice noodles, boil them in water for about 7 minutes, until cooked through. Drain, flush with cold water, and drain again. Transfer to a large plate or small baking sheet. Toss with the 1 teaspoon oil, then spread out to dry and cool completely, about 15 minutes. The noodles can be refrigerated up to 3 days; warm up to room temperature before seasoning and frying.

When starting with fresh rice noodles, do your best to separate the noodles into strands or layers (they may be sticky or hard). Set aside.

Prep the topping ingredients so you're ready to stir-fry after deep-frying the noodles. Then, to make the batter, whisk together the flour, cornstarch, baking powder, baking soda, salt, and sugar in a bowl. Whisk in the water to create a smooth, somewhat pasty batter. Set by the stove.

Use a large wok or deep skillet to fry the noodles. Pour in oil to a depth of 1 inch (2.5 cm). Heat over high heat to just under 375°F (190°C). Set a cooling rack on a baking sheet and place next to the stove.

When the oil nears temperature, lightly coat the noodles in batter. To avoid doughy noodle fritters, spread the noodles out on a plate or baking sheet. Pour on the batter. Use fingers to coat and separate them into loose piles. Things will look messy.

Fry the noodles by the small handful, gently dropping them into the oil. Aim for somewhat flat shapes (use chopsticks to spread them out). Fry for 2 to 3 minutes, turning occasionally, until crisp and golden. Drain on the rack and return the oil to temperature to fry more.

Once fried, the noodles remain crisp for a good 30 minutes, leaving you plenty of time to stir-fry the topping. Arrange the noodles on a serving plate and top with the stir-fry. Enjoy immediately.

Notes Fried noodles may be reheated in a 400°F (200°C) oven for 3 to 5 minutes, until gently sizzling and hot.

gà xào nấm

CHICKEN, MUSHROOM, AND BOK CHOY

Serves 4 to 6
with panfried
or deep-fried
noodles

Takes 30 minutes

In this noodle topping, chicken breast is enlivened by lots of zippy ginger, earthy mushroom, and jade-green bok choy. If you enjoy ginger, increase the amount to 1 inch (2.5 cm); you may be generous because it mellows during cooking.

Fresh shiitake can be pricey, so consider using both shiitake and white mushrooms to save money and lend extra complexity to the dish. Buy green-stemmed Shanghai baby bok choy, as it is tender and pretty; it's sold at many markets as well as farmers' markets.

8 ounces (225 g) boneless, skinless chicken breast, cut across the grain into slices 3 inches (7.5 cm) long and ¼ inch (6 mm) thick

⅛ teaspoon white pepper

¼ teaspoon sugar

Scant 3 teaspoons cornstarch

½ teaspoon toasted sesame oil

2 teaspoons regular soy sauce

¼ teaspoon dark soy sauce or dark molasses (optional, for rich color)

Generous ¾ cup (180 ml) broth from Quick Chicken Pho (page 40), Pressure Cooker Chicken Pho (page 46), or Classic Chicken Pho (page 59)

Fish sauce

Fine sea salt

Chubby ¾-inch (2 cm) section ginger, peeled and cut into fine matchsticks

½ medium (3 oz | 90 g) red or yellow onion, cut along the grain into thick wedges

8 ounces (225 g) baby bok choy, cut on the diagonal into pieces about ¾ inch (2 cm) wide

6 ounces (180 g) large fresh shiitake and/or regular white mushroom, trimmed and cut into thick slices

2½ tablespoons chicken pho fat, canola oil, or other neutral oil

In a bowl, combine the chicken, white pepper, sugar, 1 teaspoon of the cornstarch, sesame oil, and soy sauces. Taste the pho broth. If needed, season with fish sauce and/or salt. In a small bowl, dissolve the remaining scant 2 teaspoons cornstarch in 1 tablespoon of the broth. Set all by the stove along with the ginger, onion, bok choy, and mushroom.

To cook the topping, heat a large wok or skillet over medium-high, then swirl in 2 tablespoons of the fat. Add the ginger and onion. Stir-fry for 30 seconds, or until fragrant. Bank the aromatics on one side.

Raise the heat to high and add the chicken, spreading it out into a single layer. Let cook, undisturbed, for about 1 minute, until the edges turn opaque. Use a spatula to flip and stir-fry the ingredients for 1 to 2 minutes, until the chicken is barely cooked through. Hold on a plate.

Reheat the pan over high. Add the remaining 1½ teaspoons fat. Add the mushroom and stir-fry for 1 to 2 minutes, until slightly soft and glistening with moisture. Add the bok choy. Cook for another minute, or until heated through and tender-crisp. Pour in the broth.

When things start bubbling, return the chicken to the pan. Stir and cook for 30 to 60 seconds to finish cooking the chicken. Restir the cornstarch slurry, then add and cook for about 30 seconds, until the sauce is smooth and thick. Turn off the heat and mound atop the panfried or deep-fried noodles on pages 118 and 120, respectively.

Notes If you don't have pho broth, mix ¼ teaspoon salt, ½ teaspoon sugar, 1½ teaspoons fish sauce, 1 tablespoon regular soy sauce, 1 teaspoon toasted sesame oil, and ¾ cup (180 ml) water. Combine the 2 teaspoons cornstarch with 1 tablespoon water for a thickening agent.

bò xào tôm
BEEF, SHRIMP, AND VEGETABLES

Serves 4 to
6 with panfried
or deep-fried
noodles

—

Takes 30 minutes

Surf-and-turf combinations like this one are festive looking and delicious tasting. They're also fun to eat because there are so many interesting flavors and textures. My husband and I often have this stir-fry atop rice noodles as a one-dish weeknight dinner or weekend lunch.

To save time or avoid rushing, prep and blanch the vegetables hours in advance; ditto with seasoning the pho broth. Marinate the beef and shrimp up to an hour before stir-frying. And when using dried pho rice noodles, boil and oil them days ahead. For an all-beef delight, use 8 ounces (225 g) meat.

2½ cups (4 to 5 oz | 115 to 150 g) broccoli florets

1 small (3 oz | 90 g) carrot, peeled and thinly sliced

½ medium (3 oz | 90 g) red bell pepper, seeded and cut into 1-inch (2.5 cm) squares

5 ounces (150 g) well-trimmed top sirloin or flank steak, cut across the grain into slices 3 inches (7.5 cm) long and ¼ inch (6 mm) thick

4 ounces (115 g) large shrimp, peeled and deveined

Scant 3 teaspoons cornstarch

¼ teaspoon sugar

½ teaspoon toasted sesame oil

¾ teaspoon fish sauce, plus more as needed

1½ teaspoons regular soy sauce, or 1 teaspoon regular soy plus ½ teaspoon dark soy (for bold color)

Generous ¾ cup (180 ml) broth from Quick Beef Pho (page 45), Pressure Cooker Beef Pho (page 49), Saigon-Style Beef Pho (page 61), or Hanoi-Style Beef Pho (page 65)

Fine sea salt

½ small (2 oz | 60 g) yellow onion, cut along the grain into narrow wedges

2 cloves garlic, chopped

2½ tablespoons beef pho fat, canola oil, or other neutral oil

Pepper

Bring a pot of water to a boil. Blanch the broccoli, carrot, and bell pepper in batches for 2 minutes each, or until tender-crisp. Drain, flush with cold water, then drain well again. Put the vegetables in a bowl and set aside.

In a bowl, combine the beef, shrimp, 1 teaspoon of the cornstarch, sugar, sesame oil, fish sauce, and soy sauce; stir to coat well. Taste the pho broth and season with fish sauce and/or salt, if needed. In a small bowl, dissolve the

remaining scant 2 teaspoons cornstarch in 1 tablespoon of the broth. Line up all of the ingredients by the stove, including the onion and garlic.

To cook the topping, heat a large wok or skillet over medium-high. Swirl in 2 tablespoons of the fat. Add the onion and garlic. Stir-fry for 30 seconds, or until fragrant. Push to one side of the pan.

Raise the heat to high and add the beef and shrimp, spreading them out into a single layer. Let cook, undisturbed, for about 1 minute to brown the beef and turn the shrimp pinkish orange. Use a spatula to flip, stir, and combine everything. Cook for 1 to 2 minutes, until the beef and shrimp are still slightly rare. Hold on a plate.

Reheat the pan over high, then add the remaining 1½ teaspoons fat. Add the vegetables. Stir-fry for about 1 minute, until heated through. Add the broth, and when it begins bubbling, return the beef and shrimp to the pan. Stir for about 1 minute to combine and finish cooking through. Restir the cornstarch slurry, then add to the pan. Stir for 15 to 30 seconds, until the sauce thickens. Take off the heat and sprinkle on the pepper. Serve atop the panfried or deep-fried noodles on pages 118 and 120, respectively.

Notes If pho broth isn't available, make a flavoring sauce with ½ teaspoon sugar, 1 tablespoon oyster sauce, 2 teaspoons fish sauce, 1 teaspoon regular soy sauce, and ¾ cup (180 ml) water. Combine the 2 teaspoons cornstarch with 1 tablespoon water for a thickening agent.

đậu phụ xào húng quế

TOFU AND THAI BASIL

Serves 4 to 6
with panfried
or deep-fried
noodles
—
Takes 40 minutes

Make this splendid noodle topping with all that Thai basil you likely have left over from your pho forays. It's simply a Thai-inspired stir-fry served atop panfried or deep-fried pho noodles. It's spectacularly good, as my vegan and omnivore recipe testers reported.

If you're unfamiliar with kaffir (*makrut*) lime leaves, they are segmented leaves with a perfume like no other. One leaf includes both segments; omit the spine when cutting. Use a sharp, thin-blade knife for the most delicate results.

10 ounces (300 g) firm or extra-firm tofu

Fine sea salt

Scant 1 cup (240 ml) Vegetarian "Chicken" Pho broth (page 53)

2 teaspoons cornstarch

1½ teaspoons sugar

Scant 1 teaspoon dark soy sauce, or ½ teaspoon regular soy sauce and ½ teaspoon dark molasses

Scant 1½ tablespoons regular soy sauce

2 tablespoons finely chopped garlic

1 large (2 oz | 60 g) shallot, thinly sliced

4 ounces (115 g) green beans, cut into pinkie-finger lengths

2 large Fresno or jalapeño chiles, quartered length-wise, seeded, and thinly cut on the diagonal

2 tender kaffir (makrut) lime leaves, cut into threadlike pieces (optional)

1 cup (about .9 oz | 25 g) lightly packed fresh Thai basil, holy basil, or mint leaves

3 to 4 tablespoons canola oil or fragrant peanut oil

Cut the tofu into generous 1-inch (2.5 cm) chunks (imagine large cherries). Place the tofu on a double layer of paper towels and season with a bit of salt. Set aside to drain, about 15 minutes.

Meanwhile, taste and *lightly* season the broth with salt. In a small bowl, dissolve the cornstarch in 1 tablespoon of the broth. For a seasoning sauce, in another bowl, stir together the sugar, dark soy sauce (or dark soy and molasses), and regular soy sauce. Set the broth, slurry, and seasoning sauce by the stove along with the tofu, garlic, shallot, green beans, chiles, lime leaf, and basil.

To make the topping, blot excess moisture from the tofu with paper towel. Heat a large wok or nonstick skillet over medium-high. Swirl in 1 to 2 tablespoons of the oil. Add the tofu (work in batches, if necessary) and panfry for 3 to 4 minutes, flipping midway, until golden brown and slightly crisp on two or three sides. When done, hold the tofu on a plate.

Reheat the wok or skillet over high. Swirl in the remaining 2 tablespoons oil. Add the garlic and shallot. Stir until aromatic, 15 to 20 seconds, then add the green beans. Stir-fry for about 2 minutes, splashing in 1 to 2 tablespoons of the broth to facilitate cooking. When tender-crisp, add the tofu. Stir to combine and cook for 1 minute to heat through.

Add the chile and lime leaf, then sprinkle on the soy sauce mixture. Stir-fry for 1 minute to combine the flavors. Pour in the remaining broth. When the mixture bubbles, restir the cornstarch slurry and then add to thicken. Throw in the basil leaves. Stir until they wilt, about 15 seconds, then take the pan off the heat and use to top panfried or deep-fried noodles on pages 118 and 120 respectively.

Notes The Vegan "Beef" Pho broth (page 56) may be subbed for the "chicken" broth; to avoid a superdark sauce, omit the dark soy sauce and use all regular soy sauce. Or, purchase a golden-hued vegetable broth.

6

PHO SIDEKICKS

How do you build a meal around pho? Add light snacks and a beverage. The perennial favorites are rice paper rolls, which are consistently better when made at home. If you're curious, make wrappers for Hanoi-style pho noodle rolls. Or, push the envelope with pot stickers that give a nod to the Viet-Chinese pho link. The salads and pickle refresh and pair well with pho dishes in the earlier chapters. Add an energizing or festive drink, depending on the occasion.

PHO POT STICKERS

Makes 24 to 30 dumplings to serve 4 to 6

Takes about 1 hour, plus 20 minutes to rest filling

While I was writing this book, a Facebook friend asked how I'd go about making a pho-like dumpling. Instead of taking the convoluted route to create a graduate-level Shanghai-style soup-filled dumpling, I chose easier pot stickers. Anyone can make them from store-bought wrappers. (If you have my *Asian Dumplings* cookbook, make fresh wrappers for an extra treat.)

The filling includes elements of pho. You'll use the same aromatics and spices, as well as a little pho broth, pho fat, and fish sauce. The dipping sauce features soy sauce, which works better with the wheat-based wrapper. These freeze well, so make some in advance and trot them out for company as an impressive snack. See Notes for a meatless option.

FILLING

2 to 3 teaspoons peeled and minced ginger (use more for lamb)

1 Fresno or jalapeño chile, seeded and finely chopped

¼ cup (about .35 oz | 10 g) finely chopped fresh Thai basil, cilantro, or mint

⅓ cup (1 oz | 30 g) finely chopped green onion, white and green parts

⅛ teaspoon pepper

¼ teaspoon fine sea salt

1 teaspoon Pho Spice Blend (page 111)

1 tablespoon fish sauce

¼ cup (60 ml) pho broth (match the ground meat used) or low-sodium chicken broth

1½ tablespoons melted pho fat or canola or other neutral oil

8 ounces (225 g) ground beef chuck, dark-meat chicken (thigh meat), or lamb

½ to 1¼ teaspoons cornstarch (optional)

SAUCE

1½ to 2 tablespoons regular soy sauce

¼ cup (60 ml) Garlic Vinegar (page 106)

3 to 5 slices Fresno or jalapeño chile, or 1 Thai chile, partially split lengthwise (optional)

24 to 30 round dumpling wrappers ("pot sticker" or "gyoza" skins)

1½ to 2 tablespoons canola or other neutral oil, plus more as needed

Make the filling and the sauce In a bowl, stir together the ginger, chile, basil (or other herb), green onion, pepper, salt, spice blend, fish sauce, broth, and fat. Taste and add extra salt, fish sauce, or spice blend to create a pho-like flavor. Add the ground meat and vigorously stir with a fork until the liquid disappears. If the mixture feels too soft to handle, add the cornstarch; the amount used depends on the meat (chicken is more moist than beef or lamb) and your preference. Cover and set aside for 20 minutes or refrigerate for up to 2 days before using.

Combine the soy sauce, vinegar, and chile for a lightly salty, tangy, spicy dipping sauce; set at the table. Line a baking sheet with parchment paper and dust with flour.

Shape and cook dumplings Lay 4 to 6 wrappers on your work surface. Brush the edges of the wrappers with water. For each dumpling, hold a wrapper in a slightly cupped hand. Use a dinner knife or teaspoon to scoop up 2 to 3 teaspoons of the filling (the amount depends on the wrapper size). Place it slightly off-center toward the upper half of the wrapper. Shape it into a flat mound and keep a knuckle's length (¾ in | 2 cm) of wrapper clear on all sides.

Create your favorite shape. Otherwise, bring up the wrapper edge closest to you to close, then press to seal well and create a half-moon. To help the dumpling sit up during panfrying, make a series of large pleats at the rim from one end to the other, firmly pressing into place. (Or, form two small pleats near the center, pressing firmly to hold.)

continued

As the dumplings are made, place them, not touching, on the prepared baking sheet. Cover finished ones with a dry kitchen towel to prevent drying.

To cook, use a medium or large nonstick skillet; if both sizes are handy, cook 2 batches at once. Heat over medium-high. Add 1½ to 2 tablespoons oil (use more for a large skillet). Add the dumplings, placing them sealed edges up in a winding circle pattern or several straight rows. Let them touch. Fry for 1 to 2 minutes, until golden or light brown (lift one to check).

Holding a lid (or piece of foil) close to the skillet as a shield, use a kettle or measuring cup to add about ¼ inch (6 mm) of water, roughly ⅓ cup (90 ml). Cover and lower the heat to medium. Let cook until the water is mostly gone, 4 to 6 minutes. After about 3 minutes, slide the lid ajar for venting.

When you hear gentle frying (most of the water is gone), uncover. Fry the dumplings for 1 to 2 minutes to crisp the bottoms. Turn off the heat. When the sizzling stops, use a spatula to transfer the dumplings to a serving plate, displaying them crisp bottoms up. Eat with the dipping sauce.

Notes To make **tofu pho pot stickers**, replace the meat with 8 ounces (225 g) super-firm tofu (such as Wildwood brand sold in vacuum-sealed packages). Blot moisture from the tofu and use the coarse *and* medium holes on a box grater to create an uneven texture. Omit the broth, as the tofu is very moist. Use a scant 1½ tablespoons regular soy sauce and bind with 1 teaspoon cornstarch. Keep other ingredients the same. Shape and cook as usual.

Assembled dumplings can be covered with plastic wrap and refrigerated for 2 hours. Cook them straight from the fridge. Or, freeze dumplings on the baking sheet, and after they're rock hard, transfer to a zipper plastic bag to store up to 3 months; partially thaw for about 15 minutes on a baking sheet dusted with flour before panfrying as instructed above.

Don't want to panfry the dumplings? Steam them over boiling water for 6 to 8 minutes, until slightly puffed and somewhat translucent. Line steamer trays with parchment paper (keep the edges uncovered for heat circulation) and lightly oil to prevent sticking.

Unused wrappers can be refrigerated for a good week (make another batch). For extra-crispy pot stickers, dip the dumpling bottoms (the spine) in lots of cornstarch before panfrying. The water added during cooking will create a lacy crisp layer on the skillet.

When making **gluten-free dumplings**, use a wheat-free soy sauce; search Vietworldkitchen.com for "How to make gluten-free pot stickers" to locate a wrapper recipe.

VEGETARIAN PHO POT STICKERS

Makes 24 to 30 dumplings to serve 4 to 6

Takes about 1 hour, plus 30 minutes to cool filling

It's hard for me to pick which I like better: the meat-filled dumplings on page 129 or these vegetable-laden pot stickers. They both channel the pho spirit well. Dried shiitake mushrooms lend savory depth, color, and texture to the filling. Weigh them if you're unsure about size. Soak them overnight for the best flavor, or see Notes for a quick soak method.

To chop the vegetables and edamame in a food processor, work with each ingredient separately, cutting it into large pea-size pieces before pulsing in the processor to a fine texture. As needed, scrape down the walls. Some chunky pieces are fine for character.

FILLING

3 medium (.7 oz | 20 g total) dried shiitake mushrooms, rehydrated, stemmed, and finely chopped (save soaking liquid if using)

1 very small carrot, peeled and finely chopped (1.5 oz | 45 g)

6 ounces (180 g) frozen shelled edamame, thawed and finely chopped

⅛ teaspoon pepper

½ to ¾ teaspoon Pho Spice Blend (page 111)

1½ tablespoons regular soy sauce

¼ cup (60 ml) broth from Quick Vegetarian Pho (page 43), Vegetarian "Chicken" Pho (page 53), or Vegan "Beef" Pho (page 56) or mushroom soaking liquid

About ¼ teaspoon fine sea salt

¼ to ½ teaspoon sugar (optional)

2 tablespoons canola or other neutral oil

1 tablespoon peeled and minced ginger

Scant 1½ teaspoons cornstarch diluted in 2 teaspoons vegetarian pho broth or mushroom soaking liquid

1 Fresno or jalapeño chile, seeded and finely chopped

¼ cup (.35 oz | 10 g) finely chopped fresh Thai basil, cilantro, or mint

⅓ cup (1 oz | 30 g) finely chopped green onion, white and green parts

SAUCE

1½ to 2 tablespoons regular soy sauce

¼ cup (60 ml) Garlic Vinegar (page 106)

3 to 5 slices Fresno or jalapeño chile, or 1 Thai chile, partially split lengthwise (optional)

24 to 30 round dumpling wrappers ("pot sticker" or "gyoza" skins)

Canola or other neutral oil, for panfrying

Make the filling and the sauce In a bowl, combine the mushroom, carrot, and edamame. In a small bowl, mix the pepper, spice blend, soy sauce, and broth (or mushroom soaking liquid). Taste and add salt and sugar for an intense pho-like flavor. Set the vegetables and sauce near the stove.

Heat a wok or large skillet over medium. Swirl in the oil. Add the ginger and cook for 10 to 15 seconds, until aromatic. Add the vegetables, stir to combine, then pour in the sauce. When gently sizzling with a little bubbling liquid in the pan, restir and add the cornstarch slurry, stirring to combine.

After the mixture firms up, turn off the heat. Stir in the chile, Thai basil (or other herb), and green onion. Transfer to a bowl and let cool completely at room temperature, about 30 minutes, before using. The filling may be made up to 2 days ahead and refrigerated.

Following the instructions for Pho Pot Stickers on page 129, make the dipping sauce, then shape and panfry the dumplings. Serve them crispy bottoms up with the sauce.

Notes To quickly rehydrate dried shiitake mushrooms, snip or hack off the stems, quarter the caps, and then soak, absorbent gill side down, in very hot or just-boiled water for 10 to 20 minutes, until plump and soft. Drain (reserving the soaking liquid, if using), squeeze, then use.

phở cuốn
FRESH PHO NOODLE ROLLS

Makes about
16 rolls to serve
6 to 8

———

Takes about
1½ hours,
plus 2 hours or
overnight for
batter to rest

You may know Truc Bach Lake in Hanoi as where John McCain was shot down during the Vietnam War, but for people in search of pho snacks, the cafés in the area comprise the epicenter of *phở cuốn*—rolls of tender rice noodle sheets filled with stir-fried beef, lettuce, and herbs. Served with *nước chấm* dipping sauce, they are a special nosh or prelude to a wonderful meal.

Cooks in Vietnam usually buy fresh pho noodle sheets from market vendors. Without such convenience nearby, I make my own, and you can, too! Shop at an Asian market or online for the starches and flour. Thai-based Erewan brand (look for the three-headed elephant logo) makes excellent tapioca starch and rice flour; regular rice flour is marked by red lettering on the plastic bags. Red Lantern wheat starch is my go-to brand. Weigh the starches and flour for the best results.

Using a blender and letting the batter rest are other keys to making these rice sheets. Another secret is a cheap, thin nonstick skillet that heats up and cools down fast; the rice sheet comes out more easily when a ten-dollar skillet is involved. Don't be afraid of banging the skillet. See Notes for a rice-paper alternative.

BATTER

¾ teaspoon fine sea salt

2 tablespoons plus 1 teaspoon (.7 oz | 20 g) wheat starch

¼ cup (1 oz | 30 g) tapioca starch

Scant 1½ cups (5.6 oz | 160 g) regular rice flour, any Thai brand such as Erewan

2⅓ cups (570 ml) very hot water, about 120°F (49°C)

¼ cup (60 ml) canola or other neutral oil, plus more as needed

FILLING AND SAUCE

10 ounces (300 g) well-trimmed beef top sirloin or flank steak

1 teaspoon cornstarch

¼ teaspoon sugar

¼ plus ⅛ teaspoon pepper

1½ teaspoons fish sauce

1½ teaspoons regular soy sauce

1½ tablespoons canola or other neutral oil

2 cloves garlic, finely chopped

⅓ cup (1.5 oz | 45 g) thinly sliced shallot

2 cups (2 oz | 60 g) butter lettuce or soft leaf lettuce, cut into narrow ribbons (omit spines)

½ cup (.35 oz | 10 g) coarsely chopped fresh cilantro leaves

½ cup (.5 oz | 15 g) coarsely chopped fresh mint leaves

1 cup (240 ml) Nuoc Cham Dipping Sauce (page 139)

Make the batter Put the salt, wheat starch, tapioca starch, rice flour, water, and oil in a blender. Whirl on high speed for about 30 seconds into a silky batter that resembles whole milk. Transfer to a bowl and set aside, uncovered, to completely cool. The batter is usable after 2 hours but performs better after resting in the refrigerator for 8 hours (it can be chilled for up to 3 days); bring it to room temperature before using. Yields about 3 cups (720 ml).

Prep the filling and sauce About 1 hour before making the rice sheets, *very thinly* slice the beef across the grain into strips about 3 inches (7.5 cm) long. Transfer to a bowl and mix with the cornstarch, sugar, pepper, fish sauce, and soy sauce. Heat a wok or skillet over medium-high. Swirl in the oil, then add the garlic and shallot. When aromatic, about 30 seconds, push to the side.

Raise the heat to high. Add the beef, spreading it out into a single layer. Let cook, undisturbed, for about 1 minute, until the edges start browning. Use a spatula to flip and stir for 1 to 2 minutes longer to finish cooking. Transfer to a plate and let cool.

continued

Meanwhile, combine the lettuce, cilantro, and mint in a bowl and set near the beef. Make the dipping sauce and set side.

Make the rice sheets and rolls Use a lightweight 8-inch (20 cm) nonstick skillet. By the stove, position an inverted baking sheet near the counter's edge; put a dishtowel underneath to protect the counter, if you like. The batter will have separated, so whisk to reblend.

Heat the skillet over medium-low heat. Smear on a tiny bit of oil with a paper towel. When hot to the touch, ladle in about 3 tablespoons of the batter. The batter should barely sizzle on contact. Swirl and shake the skillet to coat the bottom; it's okay if you don't evenly coat.

Cover and cook for 60 seconds, or until translucent, bubbly, and domed up—signs of doneness. Keeping the burner on (you'll reuse it soon), slide the skillet to a cool burner.

After the rice sheet stops quivering and bubbling, about 30 seconds, run a silicone spatula around the rim. Take a breath and, with confidence, turn the skillet over and slam it onto the baking sheet. Wait for 1 to 2 seconds before checking if the rice sheet has fallen out.

Troubleshooting *Craters on the surface* mean the skillet overheated; lower the heat or briefly rest the skillet on a cool burner before trying again. *Cracks in the rice sheets* may reflect too much batter (use a little less in the pan) or batter that is too thick (add water by the teaspoon). *If the rice sheet doesn't fall out* after 3 to 5 seconds, reheat the skillet on the burner for 20 seconds, or until the sheet redomes; cool briefly, then try inverting the skillet again. *When the rice sheet falls out and is wrinkled,* use fingers to quickly straighten it out; tiny wrinkles can be hidden in the roll. Fold over dry edges, if needed. If it's a hopeless ball of rice, discard and move on to make another one. There's plenty of batter.

Once the rice sheet has cooled to lukewarm, about 45 seconds, fill it; it will self-seal if still warm and tacky. Arrange about 3 tablespoons of the lettuce, cilantro, and mint below the midline, then add some beef. Roll it up and place on a platter or baking sheet. Repeat to make more; you'll develop a rhythm. Keep rolls covered to prevent drying.

To serve, cut the rolls in half crosswise and present on a platter or individual plates. Offer with the dipping sauce. Invite guests to drizzle the sauce into the rolls or to dip into individual sauce bowls.

Notes If your tap water isn't hot enough, combine 1:1 luke-warm and just-boiled water to arrive at very hot water.

Covered with plastic wrap, filled rolls may sit at room temperature for about 2 hours before serving; refrigeration hardens them a touch.

Instead of stir-fried beef, use 10 ounces (300 g) sliced cooked meat (such as chicken, beef, or lamb from pho), or try Pan-Seared Tofu (page 97) and serve with the vegetarian version of the dipping sauce (see Notes, page 139). To make yellow or pink rolls, color the batter with ¼ teaspoon ground turmeric or 1 teaspoon beet powder, respectively.

To bypass DIY rice sheets, use about a dozen 8-inch (20 cm) rice paper rounds. Moisten a rice paper as instructed in the rice paper rolls recipe (see opposite). Once the rice paper is tacky, fill with the lettuce, herbs, and beef. Cut each roll into 2 or 3 pieces and serve. Rice paper yields chewy-tender rolls, whereas fresh pho noodle rolls are delicately tender.

gỏi cuốn
RICE PAPER SALAD ROLLS

Makes 16 rolls to serve to 6 to 8

Takes about 1 hour, plus 5 to 30 minutes to make dipping sauce

Pho is a great one-dish meal, but it's an extra treat with a side of rice paper rolls. They're light, and easy. Their name literally means "salad roll," since elements of Viet composed salads (*gỏi*) are rolled (*cuốn*) in rice paper.

This recipe combines shrimp and pork, a classic crowd-pleaser. However, you may fill these rolls many ways: Replace the pork with cooked beef or chicken from a batch of pho, use leftover grilled meats or vegetables, vary the fresh herbs according to season. Try slices of Pan-Seared Tofu (page 97) and seared fresh shiitake mushroom for a meatless version.

The devil's in the details with these rolls. The filling components should be soft and thin so they'll be easy to roll up in the rice paper sheath; and pretty rolls result from strategically placing the filling (the instructions below tell you how). Prep the filling items up to 2 days in advance, then make the rolls a few hours before guests arrive. Better yet, set up a roll-your-own station, do a demo, and let guests dive in.

FILLING

5 to 6 ounces (150 to 180 g) dried rice vermicelli noodles (see Notes)

1 teaspoon fine sea salt

8 ounces (225 g) medium shrimp, peeled and deveined (about 24 total)

6 ounces (180 g) boneless pork shoulder or pork loin chop (about the size of your palm)

1 head butter lettuce, leaves separated

12 to 16 sprigs cilantro

12 to 16 sprigs mint

16 (8 in | 20 cm) rice paper rounds (see Notes)

1⅓ cups (330 ml) Spicy Hoisin Sauce (page 138), or 1 cup (240 ml) Nuoc Cham Dipping Sauce (page 139)

Ready the filling Boil the noodles in a pot of water for 3 to 5 minutes, until chewy-soft. Drain, quickly rinse, then set aside to drain and cool to room temperature.

Fill a 1½-quart (1.5 l) saucepan half full with water, add the salt, and bring to a boil over high heat. Add the shrimp, slide the pan off heat, and let stand for 3 to 5 minutes, until the shrimp have curled up and are pinkish orange. Use a slotted spoon to transfer to a plate and let cool.

Return the water to a boil, then drop in the pork. When bubbles form at the edge of the pan, move it from the heat

and cover. Let stand for 20 minutes to gently poach. The pork should be firm yet yield a bit to the touch; cool on a plate. Save the light stock for another use (such as the spicy hoisin sauce) or discard.

To make the shrimp lie flat, cut each one into symmetrical halves. Lay it flat on a cutting board and cut in half horizontally: use the index and middle fingers of one hand to steady the shrimp as you wield the knife in a sawing motion with the other hand. Set aside on a plate.

Cut the pork across the grain into thin strips about ⅛ inch (3 mm) thick and 4 inches (10 cm) long. Add to the shrimp. Wash and prep the lettuce, cilantro, and mint; keep separate.

Set up a wrapping station Use a flat work surface (a cutting board or inverted baking sheet) and a shallow, wide bowl filled with very warm water (a little hotter than bath water since it will cool as you work) to a depth of 1 inch (2.5 cm). Place the shrimp, pork, noodles, and vegetables nearby.

Slide a rice paper round into the water to wet both sides, then place on your work surface. (Don't soak the rice paper in water or it may later fall apart.) When the rice paper is pliable and tacky (about 1 minute), fold a lettuce leaf in half

continued

along its central spine and then tear off the spine. Place the folded leaf on the lower third of the rice paper round. Put an egg-size mound of noodles atop the lettuce, spreading it into a rectangle. Top with a few mint and cilantro leaves, then add 1 or 2 pork strips.

Bring up the lower edge of the rice paper to cover the filling. Roll like a cigar upward so the lettuce faces you. Add 3 shrimp halves, cut side facing up, to the unrolled portion of rice paper; line the shrimp up snugly along the partially finished roll. Fold in the sides of the rice paper to cover the filling. Finish by rolling upward, jelly roll–style, to create a snug cylindrical package. The rice paper is self-sealing.

Repeat to make 16 rolls total, placing the finished rolls on a serving platter; cover to prevent drying. Keep at room temperature for up to several hours before serving with the sauce. Invite guests to dip the rolls into the sauce or spoon sauce onto the rolls.

Notes For the rice vermicelli noodles (also called *bún* in Vietnamese, *maifun* in Chinese, and rice sticks), look in a supermarket's Asian food aisle or the dried noodle section at an Asian market. They may appear as wiry, skinny slabs or narrow sticks. Noodles the size of angel hair pasta and made of only rice, water, and maybe salt work best for the rolls. If there's starch, they often cook up slippery and are hard to manipulate.

Rice paper is sold at many supermarkets in the Asian food aisle, conveniently shelved near the rice noodles. Use the brand that's available. At an Asian market where there's greater selection, pay at the higher end for a good brand, such as Three Ladies.

tương
SPICY HOISIN SAUCE

Makes about 1⅓ cups (330 ml)

Takes 15 minutes, plus 20 minutes to cool

Viet cooks have many approaches for making the dipping sauce to go with Rice Paper Salad Rolls (page 135). For years, my favorite rendition involved liver for an earthy edge. But with homemade pho broth and hoisin sauce in the kitchen, I came up with a knockout new version (see photo, page 137). It's lighter in flavor yet also complex thanks to the DIY ingredients and a stealth ingredient—fragrant virgin coconut oil. Regular cooking oils lack the tropical sweet lilt, though you may substitute canola oil in a pinch.

2 tablespoons creamy peanut, almond, or sunflower seed butter, with or without salt

About ⅓ cup (90 ml) Homemade Hoisin (page 102) or purchased hoisin

2 tablespoons plus 2 teaspoons water

1¼ teaspoons cornstarch

1 tablespoon virgin coconut oil

1 clove garlic, put through a press or minced and mashed with a knife

¼ to ½ teaspoon dried red pepper flakes

1 cup (240 ml) lightly salted pho broth of choice or low-sodium chicken or vegetable broth

About 1 teaspoon fish sauce or regular soy sauce, as needed

2 tablespoons finely chopped unsalted roasted peanuts, 1 teaspoon toasted sesame seeds, or mixture of both (optional)

In a small bowl, whisk together the peanut butter, hoisin, and 2 tablespoons of the water. In a separate container, stir together the cornstarch with the remaining 2 teaspoons water. Set aside.

In a small saucepan, combine the coconut oil, garlic, and pepper flakes over medium-low heat. When the oil is sizzling, fragrant, and gorgeous yellow-orange, add the hoisin mixture, whisking to combine. Whisk in the broth.

Raise the heat slightly and bring to a vigorous simmer. Let cook for 1 minute to meld flavors. Lower the heat a bit, restir the cornstarch slurry, and then whisk it into the broth mixture. Cook for 15 to 30 seconds, or until thickened. Remove from the heat and let cool to lukewarm (about 20 minutes), uncovered, to concentrate the flavors; occasionally stir to prevent a skin from forming.

Taste and add the fish sauce (or soy sauce) if a savory note is needed. Whisk in an extra teaspoon of hoisin if it's too mellow. It should taste slightly sweet, rich, and savory. Don't fear adjusting it. It's rather elastic.

When satisfied, transfer to a bowl, garnish with the peanuts and/or sesame seeds, if using, and let guests serve themselves. Or, divide the sauce among individual dipping sauce bowls and then garnish.

Notes The sauce may be prepared up to 3 days in advance and refrigerated. Warm in a saucepan over medium-low heat, adding a small splash of water to loosen, if needed. To fix a thin sauce, bring to a boil and thicken with ½ teaspoon cornstarch diluted in 1 teaspoon water. Leftover sauce may be used to dress salads and as a dip for raw or cooked vegetables.

No broth handy? Substitute 1 cup (240 ml) of the light stock leftover from poaching proteins for Rice Paper Salad Rolls (page 135). If needed, hoisin buying tips are on page 26.

nước chấm
NUOC CHAM DIPPING SAUCE

**Makes about
1 cup (240 ml)**

Takes 5 minutes

Because ingredients and palates vary, approach making Vietnam's ubiquitous, multipurpose dipping sauce by breaking it into stages. First, make a mild simple syrup. Then add the tartness, followed by the savoriness of fish sauce. Finish with heat and/or pungency. Layering on the ingredients, rather than stirring things together all at once, allows you to understand how Vietnamese flavors get built. In no time, you'll make this sauce (see photo, page 132) without a recipe. A vegetarian version is in Notes.

2½ tablespoons sugar

½ cup (120 ml) warm water

¼ cup (60 ml) fresh lime juice

2 teaspoons unseasoned Japanese rice vinegar (optional)

3 to 4 tablespoons fish sauce

1 to 2 Thai or serrano chiles, thinly sliced

1 large clove garlic, minced (optional)

Notes For a **vegetarian nuoc cham**, in a small bowl, stir and mash together a rounded ½ teaspoon fine sea salt, 3 tablespoons packed light brown sugar, and 3 tablespoons fresh lime juice. Taste and add more brown sugar or up to 1 teaspoon unseasoned Japanese rice vinegar to round out the lime juice. Add ⅔ cup (150 ml) lukewarm water and 1½ teaspoons regular soy sauce (avoid a dark sauce by using light-colored soy). Finish with 1 or 2 thinly sliced Thai or serrano chiles and 1 minced garlic clove. Serve just as usual.

In a small bowl, dissolve the sugar in the water. Taste and make sure it's pleasant to your palate; some people favor lots of sweetness so mix in extra sugar, if you like. Add the lime juice. Retaste and if there's an unpleasant tart-bitter edge, add the vinegar to round out and bridge flavors.

Add the fish sauce, starting out with 3 tablespoons and then adding more as your palate dictates, balancing the sour, sweet, and salty. How much fish sauce you use depends on the brand and your own taste.

Aim for a light honey or amber color and a bold, forward finish. Keep in mind that this sauce is typically used to dress dishes that include *unsalted* ingredients like lettuce and herbs—things that will need an extra flavor lift. Let the sauce finish a little gutsy. When you're satisfied, add the chile and garlic (if using). If diners are sensitive to chile heat, serve the chile on the side.

Put the sauce on the table so guests may help themselves, or portion it out in advance for serving. It may be prepared early in the day and kept at room temperature until serving.

gỏi bắp cải chay
CASHEW, COCONUT, AND CABBAGE SALAD

**Serves 4 to 6
as a side dish**

**Takes
20 minutes**

Pretty and bright, this vegan salad incorporates coconut's lushness by way of toasting unsweetened coconut chips (large flakes of dried coconut) with flavorful virgin coconut oil. It's a handsome side that refreshes the palate—a perfect pairing for any of the main dishes in this book as well as the pot stickers on pages 129 and 131. Feel free to prep the ingredients hours in advance and toss at the last moment.

DRESSING

2 medium limes

Unseasoned Japanese rice vinegar, as needed

1½ tablespoons sugar

1½ tablespoons regular soy sauce

1½ tablespoons canola or other neutral oil

¼ teaspoon fine sea salt

⅛ teaspoon pepper

1 small or ½ large jalapeño or Fresno chile, seeded and finely chopped

SALAD

1 teaspoon virgin coconut oil (optional)

⅔ cup (1.5 oz | 45 g) toasted unsweetened coconut chips

½ cup (2.5 oz | 75 g) salted, roasted cashews, halves and pieces

2½ cups (7 oz | 210 g) packed shredded red cabbage

1½ cups (5 oz | 150 g) matchstick-cut jicama (½ small jicama)

3 tablespoons finely chopped fresh cilantro, mint, Vietnamese coriander (rau răm), Thai basil, or a mixture

Make the dressing Use a Microplane or other fine-rasp grater to zest the limes, letting the fragrant peel drop into a large mixing bowl. Juice the limes to yield ¼ cup (60 ml); add a little vinegar if you're short. Add the juice to the zest along with the sugar, soy sauce, and oil. Stir to dissolve the sugar. Season with salt and pepper to create a balanced, savory-tangy note. When satisfied, add the chile. Set aside.

Make the salad Put the coconut oil (if using for extra flavor) and coconut chips in a skillet. Stir over medium heat for 4 to 5 minutes, until the coconut has slightly darkened and glistens (if the oil was used). Cool in a shallow bowl.

Replace the skillet on the burner and add the cashews. To refresh their flavor, toast over medium-low heat for about 2 minutes, stirring constantly, until faintly fragrant; a few dark brown spots are okay. Slide off heat to cool completely before adding to the coconut.

To serve, toss the cabbage, jicama, and herbs with the dressing. The vegetables should slightly soften and look compacted in about 60 seconds. Add the coconut and cashews. Toss well and transfer to a plate or shallow bowl, leaving any excess dressing behind. Serve.

Notes Coconut chips are often sold at health food stores in the bulk bins. If starting from untoasted coconut chips, cook them for about 7 minutes in the skillet with the coconut oil. Use medium heat, stirring frequently. After a few chips show a bit of golden brown, around the 5-minute mark, lower the heat to coax even cooking without burning. When done, the coconut chips should be golden brown and fragrant.

gỏi bắp cải gà
SPICY CHICKEN SLAW

**Serves 4 as a
side dish**

—

**Takes
20 minutes**

A great way to use leftover cooked chicken from a pot of pho is to feature it in a salad. This one is a favorite. You've likely seen it at Vietnamese restaurants. It's easy and versatile (I've provided two dressing options). For a meatless version, substitute Pan-Seared Tofu (page 97) for the chicken and add a small handful of roasted cashews.

The salad may be prepped hours in advance (chill the vegetables and chicken; keep the dressing at room temperature) and tossed before serving. You can save time by using 8 ounces (225 g) of a precut coleslaw mixture of cabbage and carrot instead of cutting up the vegetables yourself.

**DRESSING OPTION 1:
ZINGY AND BRIGHT**

1 Thai or small serrano chile, chopped

½ clove garlic

1 pinch salt

¼ to ½ teaspoon sugar

1 to 1½ tablespoons fish sauce

3 tablespoons unseasoned Japanese rice vinegar

**DRESSING OPTION 2:
EARTHY AND
SLIGHTLY SWEET**

Scant ⅓ cup (90 ml) Ginger Dipping Sauce (page 107)

SLAW

¼ small red onion or 1 shallot, thinly sliced (1 oz | 30 g)

3 to 4 tablespoons distilled white vinegar

4 ounces (115 g) cooked chicken breast from Quick Chicken Pho (page 40), Pressure Cooker Chicken Pho (page 46), or Classic Chicken Pho (page 59)

2 cups (6 oz | 180 g) packed shredded green cabbage

1 small (3 oz | 90 g) carrot, peeled and cut into thin matchsticks or shredded on largest holes of a box grater

2 tablespoons finely chopped fresh mint, Vietnamese coriander (rau răm), cilantro, or a mixture

2 tablespoons fried onion, fried shallot, or chicken cracklings (see Notes)

Make the dressing For the zingy and bright one, use a mortar and pestle to mash the chile, garlic, salt, and sugar into a fragrant, slightly sticky paste; or use a knife to mash and crush the ingredients. Transfer to a small bowl and stir in the fish sauce and vinegar. For the earthy and slightly sweet one, make the gingery sauce as directed in its recipe. Set the dressing aside.

Make the slaw To reduce the harshness of the onion (or shallot), soak it in a small bowl with distilled vinegar to cover for about 10 minutes. Meanwhile, hand shred the chicken breast along its grain into small pieces. Put in a mixing bowl along with the cabbage, carrot, and herb of choice. When the onion (or shallot) is done soaking, drain well (no need to rinse it), then add to the bowl of chicken and vegetables.

Toss the vegetables and chicken with the dressing. Things should soften and wilt slightly. Taste and adjust flavors before transferring to a serving dish; leave unabsorbed dressing behind. Garnish with fried onion, fried shallot, or chicken cracklings, then serve.

Notes For **cracklings**, after making chicken pho, remove the skin from half or all of the bird, then cut into thumb-size pieces. Gently fry over medium-low heat in a skillet or saucepan, stirring occasionally, until golden crisp. Partially cover if it spits too much; add salt, if you like. Use a slotted spoon to transfer to paper towels to cool and drain; use the same day, or refrigerate for up to 2 days.

dưa giá
PICKLED BEAN SPROUTS

Makes 2½ cups
(10 oz | 300 g)

—

Takes
20 minutes

If you like adding bean sprouts to pho, you may have extra for this bright pickle. Its tangy crunch cuts rich, salty flavors. I like to have it alongside Pho Fried Rice (page 77), and I also tuck it into Beef Pho Banh Mi (page 89). It also pairs well with the pho pot stickers in this chapter.

Heinz distilled white vinegar lends a balanced tang to this pickle, which loses its personality after 2 hours of sitting. Make it and eat it up as a hybrid pickled salad.

¾ teaspoon fine sea salt

¼ cup (1.75 oz | 50 g) sugar

½ cup (120 ml) distilled white vinegar

½ cup (120 ml) water

8 ounces (225 g) bean sprouts

⅔ cup (2 oz | 60 g) matchstick-cut carrots

2 medium green onions, green part only, cut into 1½-inch (3.75 cm) lengths

In a small saucepan, combine the salt, sugar, vinegar, and water. Stir over medium heat until the sugar and salt dissolve, then take off heat and let cool completely.

Put the bean sprouts, carrot, and green onion in a bowl (a deep one works better than a shallow one). Pour the cooled brine over the vegetables. Use fingers to toss; the vegetables won't yet be covered by brine. Set aside for about 15 minutes, turning the vegetables two or three times to expose them to the brine.

The pickle is ready when the vegetables are nearly covered by the brine, taste pleasantly tangy, and feel crunchy-soft. Keep in the brine up to 10 minutes longer, if needed. Drain and use within 2 hours.

VIETNAMESE COFFEE PRIMER

Vietnamese coffee distinguishes itself via its quirky little filter, strong-tasting coffee, and sweetened condensed milk. Here is some foundational know-how for your coffee adventure.

Phin Filter

Called *phin cà-phê* in Vietnamese, this inexpensive, low-tech coffee maker is sold at Chinese and Vietnamese markets, as well as online at Amazon. There are two kinds: one with a screw-on screen and another with a press-on screen that's gravity fed. Both work well and may be made from stainless steel or aluminum. A filter with little handles on the side is easier to pick up when hot.

The traditional *phin* filter can be slow (up to 10 minutes for a cup), but it creates a lusty, rustic, bold cup of coffee that perfectly meshes with sweetened condensed milk. It comes in different sizes, the most common one is a single-serving ¾-cup (180 ml) size. Larger ones can be found online.

If you don't have a *phin* filter, use an Aeropress or make cold-brewed coffee (instructions are on page 146), or employ a favorite method to make an inky, slightly bitter cup.

Coffee

Inexpensive ground canned coffee generally works well. At a Viet or Chinese market, look for Trung Nguyen coffee; its Premium Blend, with butter and cocoa flavoring added, lends a nice caramel-like edge. Another favorite brand is Café Du Monde with chicory, sold at Asian grocers, mainstream markets, and retailers like Cost Plus World Market.

When neither is available, try a medium-dark or dark roast, such as dark-roast Yuban or French or Spanish roast coffee. The Vietnamese *phin* filter likes a medium or medium-coarse grind coffee. Since the coffee used is often canned, the grind is predetermined.

Water

Use filtered water for your coffee, just as you would for pho. I boil water in an electric kettle, turn it off, and wait until the bubbling action stops before using. I'm not overly fussy about temperatures.

Sweetened Condensed Milk

Rich and milky sweet Longevity Brand (aka the Old Man) is the go-to brand for Vietnamese coffee. It's sold at Chinese and Vietnamese markets. At mainstream markets, select full-fat Eagle Brand, which perfectly matches Longevity's flavor. Once opened, transfer sweetened condensed milk to an airtight container. Keep it refrigerated for a good month or freeze it for up to 3 months. Bring it to room temperature to use.

cà-phê
VIETNAMESE COFFEE

Makes a generous ½ cup (120 ml)

Takes 5 to 10 minutes, depending on the coffee

At the heart of Vietnamese coffee drinks is strong coffee, a reflection of the country's coffee production of mostly punchy robusta beans. No wonder people naturally went for drinking it with sweetened condensed milk.

This recipe requires a traditional single-serving *phin* filter (see primer, page 145). It takes extra time, but the slow drip is also a gentle reminder to slow down; you're forced to wait. The amount of time depends on the coffee: Trung Nguyen and Café Du Monde take longer than others. Feel free to experiment with quantities, starting with the ratio of coffee and water below. Aeropress and cold-brewing instructions are in Notes.

2½ tablespoons ground medium-dark or dark roast coffee, such as Trung Nguyen and Cafe Du Monde with chicory

⅔ cup (150 ml) very hot or just-boiled water

Remove the screen from the filter chamber. Add the coffee, gently shaking the filter side to side to distribute. If there's a screw in the chamber, its tip should just slightly protrude. Set the filter on a cup; use a glass to monitor progress.

Place the screen atop the coffee, pressing down slightly to make sure it's sitting flat. If needed, attach the screen to the screw with a tiny turn; the attached screen should wobble ever so slightly to give the coffee room to bloom and let water pass through.

Add about 3 tablespoons of hot water to come one-fourth to one-third of the way up the exposed part of the chamber. Wait about 30 seconds, until most of the water (or all of it) has passed through.

Fill the filter chamber with the remaining water (about ½ cup | 120 ml) to just below the rim. Put the lid on and wait for the water to drip all the way through, 3 to 10 minutes.

Check occasionally. If things are not moving well, loosen the screen to release pressure and pass more water through. If there's a catch in the screen, use the edge of a spoon.

When all of the water has passed through, set the filter aside. It typically sits well atop the lid. Enjoy the coffee at a temperature that suits your needs.

Notes When using an **Aeropress**, it is fine to employ the same kind of coffee you'd put into a *phin* filter; the key is to use a little more than usual. Assemble the press with a screen or paper filter. Add 3 tablespoons ground coffee, then shake the chamber to distribute. Pour in 3 tablespoons of the hot water to moisten and bloom the coffee. After the water passes through, about 30 seconds, add the remaining ½ cup (120 ml) hot water. Stir five times, then wait for the water to pass through until half of the original volume remains, 30 to 90 seconds. Slowly plunge to express the remaining coffee to make a single serving. Aeropress coffee is smoother than *phin* coffee but lacks its attractive, edgy character.

Cold-brewed coffee is a natural for iced Viet coffee drinks and also convenient for spur-of-the-moment *cà-phê* fixes. Use a medium-coarse grind coffee like you would for the *phin* filter and a 1:4 ratio of coffee to water. For example, put ¾ cup (2.3 oz | 70 g) ground coffee and 3 cups (720 ml) filtered water in a quart-size glass or plastic container. Stir to moisten the coffee, then cover and let sit at room temperature for 12 to 24 hours. Filter through a paper coffee filter to yield about 2 cups (480 ml). Keep refrigerated for up to 3 weeks. Use cold or at room temperature. In a pinch, warm it for hot drinks.

cà-phê sữa đá
VIETNAMESE ICED COFFEE WITH CONDENSED MILK

Makes 1 drink

—

Takes 5 to 10 minutes, depending on how the coffee is made

A bowl of steamy pho and a glass of iced coffee is an unbeatable Viet food pairing. The former is nuanced and soothing while the latter is intense and energizing. Balancing dualities is part of Vietnamese culture.

Follow the recipe below the first time out. The coffee and milk are intentionally strong because ice will dilute the mixture in the glass. Once you know how much sweetened condensed milk you like, put it directly into the cup or glass that you brew the coffee in. If you worry about the ice watering things down too fast, use room-temperature or cold coffee, such as the cold-brewed coffee on the opposite page.

Generous ½ cup (120 ml) Vietnamese Coffee (see opposite)

2 tablespoons sweetened condensed milk

4 or 5 regular-size ice cubes

Make the coffee, if you haven't already, and let it briefly cool to lukewarm.

Stir together the coffee and sweetened condensed milk. Put the ice in a tall glass. Pour the coffee over the ice. Stir with a long spoon or chopstick to chill and slightly dilute before drinking.

Notes For **hot Vietnamese coffee with condensed milk**, use up to 50 percent less sweetened condensed milk. If needed, add a splash of hot water to balance flavors.

To cleanse your palate after iced coffee, try a glass of iced mild jasmine tea. The chaser can be served separately (more civilized) or it can be poured into the empty coffee glass (the leftover ice will chill the tea).

A rectangular "regular-size" ice cube, made in an old-fashioned tray, is about 2 tablespoons. The amount of ice used depends on your preference on dilution and how much you can fit into the glass.

cà-phê dừa
COCONUT COFFEE

Makes 1 drink

—

Takes 5 to
15 minutes,
depending on
how the coffee
is made

Amy Do, a young woman whom I met on a flight to Hanoi, not only volunteered her adoptive mom to give me a homemade pho lesson but also introduced me to a terrific new Viet coffee drink: coconut coffee. She took me to an outpost of Cong Caphe, a coffee-house chain that attracts young customers with well-made drinks, cool music, and an edgy parody of the socialist era (propaganda posters and militaristic staff uniforms). We exchanged emails, and with her assistance, I re-created the tropical coffee at home. There's a coconut slushie involved, so don't make the mistake of drinking this too fast unless you want a brain freeze.

Generous ½ cup (120 ml)
Vietnamese Coffee
(page 146)

Small pinch of fine sea salt

1 to 1½ teaspoons sugar

1½ tablespoons sweetened
condensed milk

3 tablespoons unsweetened
coconut milk

5 regular-size ice cubes

Brew the coffee. When it's done, stir in the salt, sugar, 1 tablespoon of the sweetened condensed milk, and 1 tablespoon of the coconut milk. Set aside. (Don't worry if the coffee becomes lukewarm or cold.)

In a blender, crush or chop the ice cubes to a fine, snowlike texture. Add the remaining ½ tablespoon sweetened condensed milk and the remaining 2 tablespoons coconut milk. Blend for about 5 seconds to combine. Scrape and spoon into a highball glass or tumbler, mounding it toward the center as a column or tall mountain.

Gently pour the coffee into the glass, aiming for the perimeter. Toward the end, the ice may float upward like a snowy glacier poking out. Serve with a spoon or chopstick for mixing.

Notes Like the iced coffee on page 147, you can use coffee that was brewed in advance. Refrigerate leftover coconut milk in an airtight container for up to 1 week (more coconut coffee!) or freeze it for up to 3 months.

SAIGON SILK

Makes 1 drink

———

Takes about
10 minutes

After sampling a pho cocktail in Hanoi (see the sidebar), I was inspired to devise some for this book. My cocktail creativity is limited, so I turned to Jeff Bareilles, a friend who has overseen the beverage programs at Manresa, Atelier Crenn, and Mourad, three of the finest restaurants in the San Francisco Bay Area where I live. Pho's botanical nature inspired Jeff to create this splendid cocktail from aromatic spirits (see photo, page 152). Fragrant gin, plum wine, and Chartreuse unite forces with bright lime juice, lively Thai basil, and anise-flavored fennel. The lime edge and Thai basil evoke Saigon-style pho.

If you don't have green Chartreuse for a stunning cocktail, use the Bénédictine and Brandy. The flavor will not be as complex but the cocktail will remain delicious. For this cocktail, you'll need a shaker and a cocktail or martini glass, coupe, or low tumbler.

3 tablespoons (1.5 oz | 45 ml)
   Tanqueray gin

3 tablespoons (1.5 oz | 45 ml)
   Takara plum wine

1½ teaspoons (.25 oz | 8 ml)
   green Chartreuse, or 1
   tablespoon (.5 oz | 15 ml)
   Bénédictine and Brandy

1 tablespoon (.5 oz | 15 ml)
   fresh lime juice

2 pinches of ground or
   pounded fennel seeds

2 bushy sprigs Thai basil,
   or 3 robust sprigs cilantro

4 regular-size ice cubes

1 lime twist

Put the gin, plum wine, Chartreuse (or Bénédictine and Brandy), lime juice, and fennel in a shaker. Use your hands to snap the herb sprigs into index-finger lengths, dropping them into the shaker. Add the ice.

Cover and vigorously shake for about 25 seconds to combine well and break down the ice. Strain into a cocktail or martini glass, coupe, or low tumbler. Add the lime twist and serve.

PHO-INSPIRED COCKTAILS

The idea seemed farfetched until Hanoi food experts Mark Lowerson and Tu Cong Van insisted that I try the pho cocktail in town. The invention of champion mixologist Tien Tiep Pham, the drink is served at the historic Hotel Sofitel Legend Metropole (he created it there as the "Joan Baez") and at the Mojito Bar & Lounge that he currently owns.

Through a multitier set of metal cups filled with pho aromatics and spices, flames fly and gin flows to pick up the essences of pho. Pham, whose résumé includes a stint at a pho stand, successfully channels the soup in his remarkable cocktail, which is garnished with chile and cilantro. Making the cocktail involved showmanship. But it didn't come off as shtick. It illustrated the creative thoughtfulness that drives Viet foodways forward.

HANOI BULLSHOT

Makes 1 drink

———

**Takes about
10 minutes**

"People cooking through your book will have lots of broth on hand, so let's make a version of the Bullshot," beverage master Jeff Bareilles said when he offered to create this delicious savory cocktail (see photo, page 152). The original drink, created around 1952 in Detroit, was basically a Bloody Mary with canned beef bouillon instead of tomato juice.

In this pho-inflected Bullshot, quick pho broth serves as the bouillon backbone; it's flavorful and lean (pho fat in a cocktail would be unpleasant). French Calvados and Luxardo liqueur amplify the broth's spice notes without adding sweetness. Hard cider injects a bright finish. Aromatics and spices echo the Hanoi pho experience. Employ leftover broth or make a batch and let it cool and chill. Before using it, taste and season the broth as if you're about to use it for noodle soup. Have a muddler (or pestle) and a double old-fashioned glass handy.

¼ medium lime

2 thin slices unpeeled ginger

8 fresh mint leaves and
    1 sprig mint

4 or 5 thin Fresno or jalapeño
    chile slices

½ cup (4 oz | 120 ml) broth
    from Quick Vegetarian Pho
    (page 43) or Quick Beef
    Pho (page 45)

¼ cup (2 oz | 60 ml) Calvados
    or apple brandy

1 tablespoon (.5 oz | 15 ml)
    Luxardo maraschino
    liqueur

4 regular-size ice cubes

2 tablespoons (1 oz | 30 ml)
    Samuel Smith organic cider
    or other dry, hard cider

1 star anise (8 robust
    points total)

Squeeze the lime wedge into a measuring cup and drop it in. Add the ginger, mint leaves, and 2 or 3 chile slices (use more for heat). Muddle and crush to release and combine the flavors. Add the broth, Calvados, and Luxardo. Briefly and gently muddle to combine.

Put the ice in a double old-fashioned glass. Strain the broth mixture into it. Add the cider. Gently rub the remaining mint sprig to release its oils before sliding it in. Drop in the remaining chile slice(s). Holding a Microplane grater over the glass, swipe the star anise about fifteen times. If you like, drop the star anise into the glass as a garnish. Serve.

Notes For the Calvados, there's no need to go top-shelf. I purchased mine at Trader Joe's. However, there's no substitute for Luxardo, which is used as a secret ingredient in many cocktails.

To make these cocktail recipes accessible to a wide audience, regular measurements as well as fluid ounces are provided. Few obstacles should stand between you and a good drink.

HANOI
BULLSHOT

SAIGON
SILK

PHO
MICHELADA

PHO MICHELADA

Makes 2 drinks

—

Takes about 10 minutes

As the last recipe in this book, this one speaks to pho's cross-cultural identity and potential. Many pho shops in America benefit from people of Mexican descent, who may be on staff and counted among their patrons. Aside from the pho connection, there is another Viet-Mexican tie: both cultures enjoy beer on ice, my initial inspiration for this riff on the *michelada* beer cocktail.

After food writer Javier Cabral told me of a restaurant in Guadalajara serving *micheladas* with a beef-tomatillo stock, the door swung open to incorporating pho broth, chile sauce, and pho spices in my cocktail. The resulting pho *michelada* is festive and easy to love, perfect for brunch or a nosh session.

As with the Hanoi Bullshot on page 151, use leftover pho broth or whip up a batch and chill it; taste and season it before using. Have the Pho Spice Blend in your pantry to give this drink a pho-ish rim. A lager-style beer lets the pho notes shine bright. You need two 1-pint (480 ml) glasses for this recipe.

1 teaspoon coarse kosher salt

¼ teaspoon Pho Spice Blend (page 111)

½ medium lime, cut into 2 wedges

½ cup (4 oz | 120 ml) broth from Quick Vegetarian Pho (page 43) or Quick Beef Pho (page 45)

¼ cup (2 oz | 60 ml) canned tomato juice, such as Campbell's

1 to 3 teaspoons Chile Sauce (page 103) or sriracha

10 regular-size ice cubes

1 (12 oz | 360 ml) bottle lager beer, such as Dos Equis or Heineken

4 slices jalapeño chile slices

On a plate, mix together the salt and spice blend. For each drink, rub a lime wedge around the rim of a 1-pint (480 ml) glass, then rim the glass with the salt and spices. Squeeze the lime wedges into a measuring cup, then add the broth and tomato juice; reserve the lime wedges. By the teaspoon, stir in the chile sauce to create a slight edge of heat.

Divide the ice between the glasses, then pour in the broth mixture. Split the beer evenly between the glasses. Stir three to five times to mix.

Use the broad side of a knife to lightly bruise the jalapeño slices to release their heat, then drop 2 slices into each glass. If you want extra tang, squeeze a reserved lime wedge over each glass to add residual drops of juice, then drop the wedge into the glass and serve.

Acknowledgments

Who knew that my lifelong relationship with pho would turn into a book? Thanks to my parents, Hoang and Tuyet Nguyen, and husband, Rory, for indulging me.

I was buoyed by the incredible enthusiasm from Ten Speed Press. Team Pho included Aaron Wehner, Hannah Rahill, editor extraordinaire Kelly Snowden, marketing maestros Michele Crim, David Hawk, and Allison Renzulli, and design guru Betsy Stromberg.

I owe a ton to an exceptional group of volunteer recipe testers, as well as their families and friends: Diane Carlson, Alex Ciepley, Jay Dietrich, Alyce Gershenson, Doug and Candace Grover, Thien-Kieu Lam, Ari LeVaux, Laura McCarthy, Hugh McElroy, Catherine McGuire, Rosemary Metzger, Alec Mitchell, Josie Nevitt, Jenny Sager, Karen Shinto, Terri Tanaka, Katherine Thome, Maki Tsuzuki, and Dave Weinstein.

Many others lent a hand. My cousins Kiet Si Nguyen, Phu Si Nguyen and his wife Hanh Thi Do, Hai Si Nguyen, and Huy Le Do offered insights as Saigon and Hanoi residents. Cuong Pham of Red Boat fish sauce prompted a pho expedition. Yun Ho Rhee shared ideas and contacts. Cynthia and Tiet Bui tracked down rare pho souvenirs.

Vietnam-based food experts Tracey Lister, Mark Lowerson, Tu Cong Van, Connla Stokes, and Dan Tran generously contributed knowledge. Erica Peters helped validate historical information. Celia Sack championed giving pho a sense of place. Uyen My Hoang, Amy Do, Nickie Tran, and Giang Van volunteered time and friendship. I've also benefited from countless kind strangers who shared their pho enthusiasm but not their names.

I'm also grateful to my Vietworldkitchen.com and social media communities: your comments, likes, and loves matter.

This book looks amazing because of art director and designer Betsy Stromberg, photographer John Lee, and food stylist Karen Shinto and her assistant, Lori Nunokawa. Not only did they bring their professionalism to showcase pho but also props for our photoshoot. Extra thanks to Karen for being a fabulous travel companion and photographer. Copyeditor and proofreader Sharon Silva and indexer Ken DellaPenta ensured that the words were as good as the images.

It takes a small, smart village to make a good cookbook. Thank you, Team Pho!

About the Author

Genevieve Pierson | Common Thread Creative

Andrea Nguyen is an author, teacher, and consultant based in the San Francisco Bay Area. Born in Vietnam, she came to the United States at the age of six. Her first book, a children's book, chronicles that journey. She has written a number of acclaimed cookbooks, including *Into the Vietnamese Kitchen*, *Asian Dumplings*, and *The Banh Mi Handbook*. Many organizations have recognized her excellent work, including the James Beard Foundation, International Association of Culinary Professional, and National Public Radio.

Andrea's food writing has appeared in the *Wall Street Journal*, *Cooking Light*, *Lucky Peach*, *Saveur*, and *Rodale's Organic Life*, where she is a contributing editor. Keep up with her at Vietworldkitchen.com.

Index

Copyright © 2017 by Andrea Quynhgiao Nguyen
Studio photographs copyright © 2017 by John Lee

Published in the United States by Ten Speed Press,
an imprint of the Crown Publishing Group, a division
of Penguin Random House LLC, New York.
www.crownpublishing.com
www.tenspeed.com

Ten Speed Press and the Ten Speed Press colophon are
registered trademarks of Penguin Random House LLC.

Vietnam location photographs courtesy of Karen Shinto.

Text from the introduction first appeared in *Lucky Peach*
magazine.

Library of Congress Cataloging-in-Publication Data

Names: Nguyen, Andrea Quynhgiao, author.

Title: The pho cookbook : from easy to adventurous,
recipes or Vietnam's favorite soup and noodles /
by Andrea Quynhgiao Nguyen.

Description: First edition. | Berkeley, California : Ten Speed
Press, [2016] | Includes bibliographical references and index.

Identifiers: LCCN 2016022687 (print) | LCCN 2016024559 (ebook)

Subjects: LCSH: Cooking, Vietnamese. | Noodle soups. | LCGFT:
Cookbooks.

Classification: LCC TX724.5.V5 N474 2016 (print) |
LCC TX724.5.V5 (ebook) | DDC 641.59597—dc23
LC record available at https://lccn.loc.gov/2016022687

Hardcover ISBN: 978-1-60774-958-5
eBook ISBN: 978-1-60774-959-2

Printed in China

Design by Betsy Stromberg

10 9 8 7 6 5 4 3 2 1

First Edition